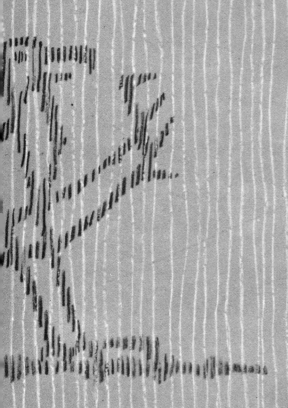

SPECIAL CONSULTANTS

THE GOLDEN TREASURY OF
KNOWLEDGE

VOLUME
9

OF SIXTEEN VOLUMES CONTAINING 420 BASIC
ARTICLES WITH 2500 ILLUSTRATIONS AND MAPS

Margaret Bevans
EDITOR-IN-CHIEF

Joanna Aldendorff
EDITORIAL CONSULTANT

Clifford Junceau
PROJECT CONSULTANT

Tom Torre Bevans
DIRECTOR

EDITORIAL STAFF
Renée Algrant · Doris Ballard · Richard Keigwin
I. W. Klein · Morgan Larkin · Henry Mins
Carol Z. Rothkopf · Peter Share

PRODUCTION STAFF
Rosalie Barrow · Frank Bologna · Ken Braren
Rosemary Gutwillig · Alan M. Heicklen
Yvonne Charles Johnson · Harris Lewine · Alice Lupo
Peter Marks · Tomaso Puliofito · Bruce Ross · Loretta Trezzo

COVER BY Ray Pioch

GOLDEN PRESS · NEW YORK

About VOLUME 9 and how it relates to other volumes

The articles in Volume 9 will take you to countries in Europe, South America, and Asia. You will learn about such things as the most nourishing and the least nourishing plants, and about doctors, explorers, and dancers.

While you read of all these things, your curiosity will grow, and you will want to investigate further. DANCE THROUGH THE AGES will lead you to ANCIENT GREEK THEATER, which will appear in a later volume. ANIMALS OF THE WORLD and their adaptation to climate will interest you in HOW ANIMALS' BODIES ARE PROTECTED farther along in the series. THE NEGRO PEOPLES OF AFRICA will make you want to know more about their countries and what is happening to them, and this you can read about in CHANGING AFRICA. THOMAS JEFFERSON will lead to other revolutionaries, such as BENJAMIN FRANKLIN. And POISONOUS PLANTS may interest you in HERBS, plants that are grown especially for medicines.

Don't stop in your search for knowledge at the end of one volume. Look in the index in Volume 16 to find more information all through the *Golden Treasury of Knowledge.*

CON[TENTS]

PA[GE]

TENTS

See page 797 for a time chart which will show how periods of history relate to one another and at what time many of the events in these articles took place.

A Short History of Astronomy

Astronomy is probably the oldest of all the sciences. Before men knew anything about biology or chemistry or physics, they learned something about astronomy by looking at the sky. They learned to measure time. They saw that the moon grows larger and smaller in a certain number of days. Men counted the passing of days and seasons and learned when to plant crops. They saw that the sun rises and sets in approximately the same place on the horizon and from this learned to find their way.

The way in which the planets and stars appear to move when we look at the sky is different from the way in which they actually do move. Early observers without instruments or mathematical knowledge knew little about what the heavenly bodies are and much less about how far away they are and how they move in relation to one another.

The earth seems gigantic to us and the sun very large. But the sun and the earth and our whole solar system are just a very small part of a vast universe in which there are billions of suns or stars, some with planets, moving in space in enormous groups.

Astronomers have tried to find out what the heavenly bodies are and to explain their movements. With the development of instruments such as the telescope, the camera, the transit, and the spectroscope, scientists have been able to see and understand some of the stars and planets. They have been able to measure and approximate the great distances between them. Beginning with Newton's theories about the laws of motion in the 17th century, scientists have been able to understand mathematically the motions of heavenly bodies. Each step in the history of astronomy has served not only to further our knowledge about the universe, but to correct earlier mistakes.

The ancient peoples, including the Babylonians, Chaldeans, Egyptians, and Greeks, believed that the heavenly bodies and what seem to be their movements influence the lives of men, and that from them one can predict the future. This belief led to astrology. For example, it was widely believed that the appearance of a comet is an omen of evil.

But these early civilizations, beginning from roughly 1,500 years before the birth of Christ, did discover some true things about the heavenly bodies. They learned about the phases of the moon and eclipses of the sun and moon. They observed that some stars seem to remain in the same place in the sky while others seem to wander about in it. The word planet is from the Greek word that means wanderer.

The Babylonians, who lived more than 2,000 years before the birth of Christ, divided the heavens into regions. They divided the groups of stars into constellations and named them after animals or gods or objects. They believed that the earth was flat. Even in the 15th century, during the time of Columbus, most people still believed the earth was flat.

Some of the early Greek astronomers thought that the earth remains in the same place in space at the center of crystal globes to

Galileo's telescope enabled him to see the surface of the moon and separate stars in the Milky Way.

The largest telescope in the world is on Mount Palomar, in California.

Radio telescopes are used to capture faint cosmic radio signals.

713

Nicolaus Copernicus discovered that the sun, and not the earth, is the center of our universe.

Johann Kepler found out that planets move in oval orbits around the sun, not in circles.

Galileo Galilei was one of the first men to use the telescope in his observations of the heavens.

Isaac Newton explained the motion of the planets by his theory of gravitation.

Edmund Halley discovered that comets repeat their paths. He was able to predict the time when one comet would reappear in the skies.

which the moon, the sun, the planets, and the stars are attached. These globes move around the earth, taking the heavenly bodies with them. But the early theories that placed the earth in the center of the universe with heavenly bodies circling around it could not completely account for the movements of the planets. So scientists continued questioning.

Even though Aristarchus of Samos in the 3rd century B.C. believed that the earth and other planets moved around the sun, it was not until 1,900 years later that this theory was accepted. Nicolaus Copernicus in the 16th century revolutionized astronomy with his theory that the sun, not the earth, is the center of the universe. He also stated that heavenly bodies rise and set because the earth rotates on its axis.

Johann Kepler, at the beginning of the 17th century, was the first to discover that the planets move in elliptical or oval orbits around the sun, not in circles. He worked out mathematical laws about the movements of the planets.

Galileo Galilei, who lived at the same time as Kepler, did much to advance the theories of

The aphelion is the point in a planet's orbit when it is most distant from the sun.

The perihelion is the point in a planet's orbit when it is nearest to the sun.

The apogee is the point in its orbit when the moon is farthest from the earth.

The perigee is the point in its orbit when the moon is nearest the earth.

The nadir and the zenith are imaginary points in space. The nadir is underfoot and the zenith is overhead.

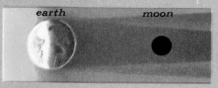

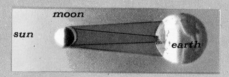

When one celestial body darkens another, it is an eclipse. Above, eclipse of the moon. Below, eclipse of the sun.

both Kepler and Copernicus. He was one of the first to use the telescope to observe the heavens. The telescope had been invented early in the 17th century. Galileo, with instruments he made himself, discovered dark spots on the sun's surface. Since the positions of the sunspots changed, he concluded that the sun also rotates on its axis. He saw that the surface of the moon is full of mountains and craters, and is not smooth as people had thought. He also discovered the four principal moons or satellites of the planet Jupiter, the phases of the planet Venus, and that the light from the Milky Way comes from millions of individual stars.

Isaac Newton published the first of his laws of motion in 1687. He explained the motion of the planets relative to the sun by his theory of gravitation. It states that all objects attract each other, and the force of their attraction depends on the weight of the objects and the distance between them. Gravity is the force that governs the movements of the planets and their satellites.

Edmund Halley, a friend of Newton's, calculated the orbits of 24 comets to see if any of them had passed twice over the same path. Based on his calculations, he was able to announce that a comet would appear in 1759, and when it did, his name was given to it. Halley's Comet has appeared about every 75 years since. Comets, like planets, do not move by chance, but according to Newton's laws of motion. Their elliptical orbits are very long and may take them tremendous distances from the sun.

Halley also checked the positions of the so-called fixed stars which Hipparchus had charted about 1,850 years before. He found that some of them had changed their positions. He thought that if some of the stars had moved, it might be true that the others, including the sun, were in motion also. This put an end to the theory that the sun is the center of the universe and placed the sun as only one star among billions of stars.

Laplace was one of the astronomers of the 18th century who studied the orbits of the planets. In England, William Herschel, in 1781, surprised the whole world by discovering the planet Uranus. Herschel also studied stars and star groups.

The last 50 years have seen some breathtaking developments in astronomy. Albert Einstein's theory of relativity set forth new ideas of time, space, motion, and gravitation. Harlow Shapley of Harvard determined the distances to the great groups of stars called globular clusters. Edwin Hubble and Milton Humason, American astronomers, used the 100-inch telescope on Mt. Wilson to study the distribution of galaxies in space. A galaxy is an enormous group of stars and our solar system is part of one galaxy.

With very powerful telescopes made with lenses or mirrors, we can see stars 2,000,000,-000 light years away. With recently made radio telescopes we can catch impulses from celestial bodies 30,000,000,000 light years away. With these radiotelescopes, scientists are now listening for intelligible signals from outer space.

Within a few years rocket ships will be able to visit the moon and the nearer planets and to explore our solar system. A new era of astronomy will then begin—the era of direct knowledge of our neighbors in the sky.

Roads

The first road was probably made by primitive men and animals who kept crossing in the same place time after time, clearing away the underbrush. Since early times new methods of transportation have made new types of roads necessary. There are now country roads where paths may have once been, and there are superhighways where country roads once were.

(1) The simplest and most primitive kind of road is a footpath. A footpath is created by the travels of men and animals over the same ground. This clears the underbrush and keeps the grass from growing.

(2) A track is a short path that can hardly be seen. A desert caravan route is a track for animals.

(3) Cattle tracks are grassy paths, hundreds of feet wide, found in plains and grazing

lands. They are used to move herds from winter to summer quarters.

(4) State highways are the main links between the cities in a state. They are paved, and divided into several lanes so that several lines of cars may travel on them. Formerly, depending on the weather, roads and streets were either muddy or dusty. Early in the 20th century, roads were covered with gravel and other weather resistant substances. When the automobile became popular, other materials such as tar and asphalt were tried because automobile tires did not spoil their surfaces. Concrete has been found to be the most practical of all road-building materials because it is weather resistant and can withstand a lot of use.

(5) County roads link smaller cities and are also paved.

(6) Community roads connect small towns and villages throughout the country. They are not always paved.

(7) Farm roads have natural surfaces made smooth by constant use. They connect farms and sometimes lead to wider roads.

(8) Country roads are even smaller than farm roads, although they serve the same purpose in non-farm areas. There are over 3,000,000 miles of rural roads in the United States, of which about 60 percent are paved in some way.

(9) Coastal roads are those that are built along lake or ocean shores.

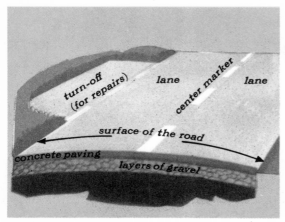

The parts and layers of a paved highway

(10) Superhighways, such as turnpikes and parkways, are the newest kind of road. They are built for travel at a higher speed than is permitted on intercity or town roads. Superhighways are generally built so that cars, trucks, and buses may go long distances at high speeds without having to stop for lights or railroad crossings. Most superhighways have limited access. That is, it is possible to get on and go off these roads only at certain specific points. There are usually several layers of materials in a superhighway, including gravelly soil and eight or 10 inches of concrete surfacing.

In an age where most short-distance travel is done by motor-driven vehicles, particularly cars and buses, it is important that roads be kept in repair. State and local governments have set up commissions to see that the roads are fit for travel.

France

The territory which is now France was first occupied by several primitive tribes. The Gauls, a Celtic race from beyond the Rhine, began to invade the rich land in about 600 B.C. The Gauls were rugged warriors, but they were constantly fighting among themselves. This made them an easy prey to the military skill of the neighboring Romans.

In 58 B.C. the Gallic tribes were engaged in one of their periodic civil wars. The Romans, under Julius Caesar, saw their chance and attacked the feuding Gauls. Within five years the whole country was in Roman hands. Gaul remained a Roman province for 500 years.

Starting about A.D. 400, western Europe was overrun by wave after wave of Germanic peoples, called barbarians by the Romans. They

A warrior of the Gauls

reached as far south as Italy and helped to overthrow the Roman Empire. Among these peoples were the Franks, who occupied most of Gaul by the end of the fifth century. They named their new country France.

The most active of the Frankish leaders was Clovis. He gained the support of the Christian church in Gaul when he had himself and his warriors baptized Christians. The existing clergy then supported him in his efforts to unify the country.

Clovis founded the Merovingian dynasty—named for a legendary Frankish king—which ruled for 250 years. But the later Merovingian kings were weak, and the power gradually shifted to the Mayors of the Palace, or seneschals, who acted as prime ministers.

Meanwhile, a new threat to France and to Christianity—the Arabs—was advancing from the east. The Arabs conquered all of North Africa, took Spain, and then crossed over the Pyrenees Mountains to France. Under the sen-

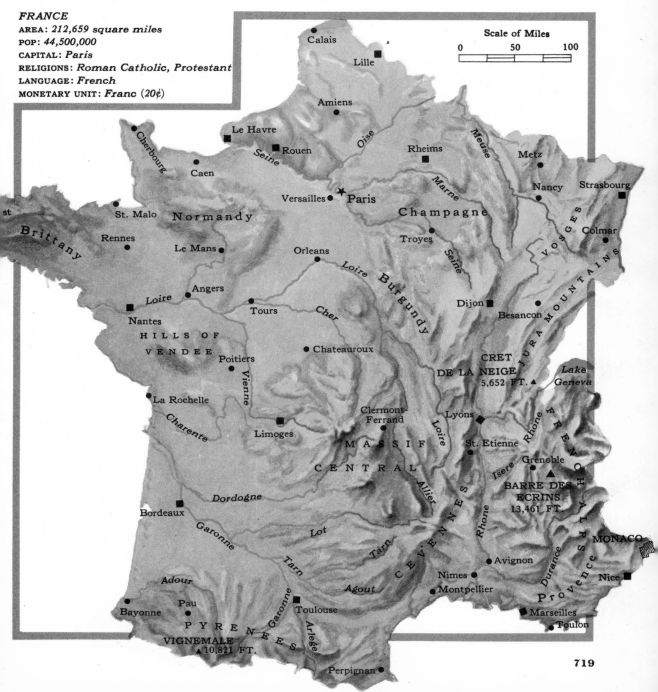

FRANCE
AREA: *212,659 square miles*
POP: *44,500,000*
CAPITAL: *Paris*
RELIGIONS: *Roman Catholic, Protestant*
LANGUAGE: *French*
MONETARY UNIT: *Franc (20¢)*

Scale of Miles
0   50   100

Calais
Lille
Amiens
Le Havre
Rouen
Seine
Oise
Rheims
Meuse
Metz
Cherbourg
Caen
Marne
Nancy
Strasbourg
Versailles
Paris
Champagne
Vosges
Colmar
St. Malo
Normandy
Troyes
Seine
Brittany
Rennes
Le Mans
Orleans
Loire
Burgundy
Dijon
Besancon
Jura Mountains
Angers
Loire
Tours
Cher
Nantes
HILLS OF VENDEE
Chateauroux
CRET DE LA NEIGE 5,652 FT.
Lake Geneva
Poitiers
Vienne
La Rochelle
Charente
Clermont-Ferrand
Lyons
Rhone
French Alps
Limoges
MASSIF
St. Etienne
Isere
Grenoble
CENTRAL
BARRE DES ECRINS 13,461 FT.
Dordogne
Allier
Bordeaux
Garonne
Lot
Rhone
MONACO
Tarn
Cevennes
Durance
Provence
Nice
Adour
Tarn
Garonne
Agout
Nimes
Avignon
Montpellier
Pau
Bayonne
Toulouse
Marseilles
PYRENEES
Ariege
Toulon
VIGNEMALE 10,821 FT.
Perpignan

eschal Charles Martel, French warriors defeated the Arabs near Poitiers in A.D. 732. For about 250 years after that, Charles and his descendants were the real rulers of France. They were the Carolingian dynasty. The greatest of the line was Charlemagne.

Charlemagne ruled from 768 to 814. He defeated all of his enemies in many great battles, and he created an empire that was as large as the old Roman Empire. He was named Holy Roman Emperor by the Pope in 800. But he did not organize any lasting system of government. 29 years after his death, his immense possessions were divided among his three grandsons. Within a few years France was again split up by small, local feuds.

The Carolingian dynasty lasted until 987, but by that time it, too, was weak. The real force in France came to rest with the nobility. Hugh Capet, a duke, was elected King and founded a new dynasty, the Capetians. The Capetians slowly gained strength, but it was not until 1200 that Phillipe Augustus began to extend the royal power. For several centuries the Capetians and their relatives, the Valois kings, fought with the barons and feudal lords for control of the country.

This battle between the king and his subjects kept France in a state of constant civil war. France also fought many wars with her neighbors, especially the English, and supported the Crusaders when they tried to recap-

Clovis I was baptized in Rheims Cathedral in 496.

Charles Martel defeated the Arabs at Poitiers.

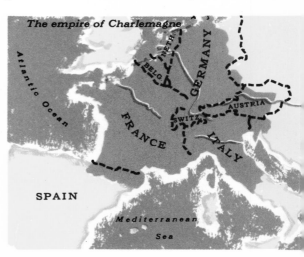

The Holy Roman Empire of Charlemagne

ture the Holy Land from the Arabs. There were some capable kings and many weak ones, but despite this the country generally prospered.

France did have periods of trouble, too, and its fortunes never seemed lower than in the early 15th century. It was divided against itself, beset by famine and disease, and involved in a long, unsuccessful war with the English. All this was changed by a young girl, Joan of Arc. Joan believed she heard voices telling her to go to Orleans, which the English were besieging. The French soldiers were fired by her courage and spirit. They followed her to Orleans, raised the siege, and drove the English from the land. At last, in 1429, Joan saw to it that the young prince of France, Charles VII, was crowned at

Rheims. When she was captured by the Burgundians in 1430 and sold to the English, she was condemned as a heretic and burned at the stake. But she had helped to unify France, which thereafter had a patriotic and united spirit that made it the leading power in Europe.

Spain and Austria did not accept France's position without a struggle. Wars were fought between the three countries for nearly 300 years. France held her own because of two able and unscrupulous ministers, Cardinal Richelieu, who served Louis XIII, and Cardinal Mazarin, who served the young Louis XIV. When Louis XIV took over personal control in 1661, France was probably the leading power in the world.

Louis XIII

Cardinal Richelieu

Louis XIV

Cardinal Mazarin

Joan of Arc led France against the English.

Louis XIV, who ruled until 1715, was the most absolute monarch of France. He controlled and directed everything, from foreign policy to the leisure activities of his subjects. He built the palace of Versailles, where the nobility played at governing under the watchful eye of the real ruler of France. He fought wars with the English, the Spaniards, and the Austrians. During his long reign there was great activity in building, art, philosophy, and science. But when he died, the people rejoiced. For Louis XIV, who liked to be called the Sun King, had impoverished his country and made it ripe for revolution.

The revolution did not come until 1789, after Louis XV, who succeeded Louis XIV, had plunged the country into a series of disastrous wars and had been succeeded by his son, Louis XVI. The revolutionists burned the Bastille, the prison that was the symbol of royal power. They executed the king and queen and many of the nobility. But they also found themselves at war with the rest of Europe. Great victories

with final victory in 1945. A Fourth Republic was declared, but conditions in France continued to be chaotic. Indo-China was lost, and a war in the French African possession of Algeria could not be completed. In 1958 de Gaulle was recalled to head the French government and given almost imperial powers. The Fifth

The French nobility danced at Versailles while their ruler, Louis XIV, impoverished the country.

The Bastille was overthrown on July 14, 1789

were won under the command of Napoleon. the Little Corporal, but by 1815 France was overwhelmed by its foes. Exhausted by war, it accepted Louis XVIII as its ruler.

The ideals of the revolution were not dead, and in 1848 the people rose again. Many Frenchmen longed for the glories of the Napoleonic period, and they soon chose a new emperor, Napoleon III. Under this Second Empire, France added greatly to her colonial possessions in Africa and southeast Asia. But then France's greatest enemy was Germany. As a result of war with Prussia, Napoleon III was overthrown, and France declared a Third Republic. This republic survived the First World War—1914 to 1918—when Germany attacked France through Belgium and the Netherlands as she had in 1870. The Third Republic ceased to exist in 1940, when the Germans invaded France for the third time in 70 years and took control of most of Europe.

Some Frenchmen did not surrender in 1940. The Free French, as they were called, under Charles de Gaulle, fought throughout the war on the side of the Allies and were rewarded

On December 2, 1804, Napoleon was proclaimed Emperor of France. At the coronation, held in the Cathedral of Notre Dame, Napoleon also crowned his wife, Josephine.

Republic was declared. For a time France has prospered. De Gaulle has proved a firm leader of divergent forces, but the problem of Algeria has not been entirely solved.

In size, France is not a large country—only a little bigger than Oregon and Nevada combined. It is one of the most powerful industrial nations in the world. But agriculture is still the most important economic activity. French soil is rich and fertile, and France raises a large wheat crop, as well as oats, potatoes, corn, sugar beets, rye, barley, and fruit. French farms tend to be small, but modern farming methods are used.

The best known French agricultural product is wine. France is the leading wine producer of the world, making about 1,000,000,000 gallons a year. Thousands of acres are planted in vineyards, and the finest French wines are considered to be among the best in the world.

France is the third leading producer of iron ore. Large deposits of bauxite, from which aluminum is made, are located in Provence, and there are also large coal deposits. Natural gas

Napoleon III, the second emperor of France

Charles de Gaulle, leader of the Free French forces in World War II

is found in the Pyrenees. The Sahara Desert—part of the French community in Africa—contains vast oil fields. France also has numerous hydro-electric installations, and has recently built modern nuclear plants.

The French iron and steel industry employs 125,000 workers. The textile industry is very important, and the silk mills of Lyons are among the most famous in the world. French mills also make woolens, cotton, and lace. The automobile industry, concentrated around Paris, is also important. Renault and Citroen cars are exported to the United States by the thousands.

Bordered by the Strait of Dover, the English Channel, the Atlantic, and the Mediterranean, France maintains a thriving trade with all the important countries of the world. She also has a modern transportation system. There is a dense network of railroads, highways, and canals.

France is primarily a nation of small towns and villages. But the capital, Paris, has a metropolitan population of more than 6,600,000. Although it is 230 miles from the sea, Paris is an important inland port. The Seine River is navigable for ships up to 800 tons all the way from the city to the sea. Paris is a commercial and industrial center as well. And it is a tourist attraction for millions of visitors each year. There are many theaters and museums, as well as beautiful public buildings.

Other important French cities are Lyons, Bordeaux, Toulouse, Marseilles—founded about 600 B.C. by Greek colonists from Asia Minor—and Nice. Nice probably was also a Greek colony, and today it is the capital of the French Riviera. The climate of Nice is mild in

winter and warm in summer, which has made it a popular resort city. Other French vacation areas are Normandy, Champagne, where famous wines are made, and the French Alps, which are beautiful all year around.

The grape harvest in Champagne, one of the leading wine producing districts of France

France carries on trade with almost all the countries of the world.

Bananas

The banana is a tropical plant—not a tree —that bears its fruit in hanging clusters. The name banana is African, but the fruit is not grown only in Africa. It grows in all parts of the tropics. Bananas are so well liked that they are in demand everywhere in the world. They are shipped by caravan, ship, airplane, and train to distant cold countries where they cannot be grown.

Bananas were cultivated in Asia for many years before they ever grew in Europe. Alexander the Great sent plants back to Greece and Rome when he returned to Persia from his expedition in India. In the beginning of the 16th century the Spaniards took the plant to the West Indies. From there it spread to Central and South America.

The plant has a grassy stem that is soft enough to be cut with a knife. It is made up of layers of leaves inside one another. The real trunk spreads along just under the surface of the ground. The roots grow downward from this trunk while the stem grows upward. A single plant may grow three or four stems in one year. Each stem will be in a different state of development. Banana plants bear flowers and fruit at the same time. As each stem fruits, it dies. Usually there are about 10 leaves to a plant. They look like palm leaves.

When the plant is 10 months old the flowers form. As the blossoms grow, the flower stalk lengthens and curves downward. The flower spike is large, with many yellow blossoms. The flowers are arranged in a half-circle cluster. They are covered with a pink substance which falls when the fruit begins to form. As the bases of the flowers fill out into fruit, they turn upward and form bunches around the stem. The bunches are called hands.

Each stem has from 10 to 20 hands of fruit. Each hand is made up of from seven to 20 fingers. A stem can have 200 or more bananas on it. The fruit is oblong, sickle-shaped, and pulpy, with no seeds. Since the banana grows from the root, no seeds are necessary. To make

A group of bananas is called a hand. The individual bananas are fingers.

How the bananas form

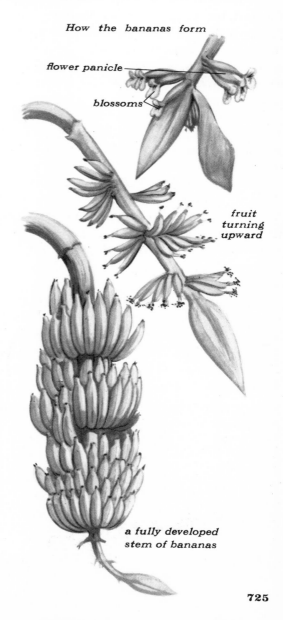

flower panicle

blossoms

fruit turning upward

a fully developed stem of bananas

The stem of a banana plant is underground. Layers of leaves form what looks like a stem.

a new plant, the rootlike trunk is cut into small pieces and planted.

There are a great many varieties of banana, but there are only two principal ones. *Musa sapientum* has fruit four to eight inches long with a soft, sweet, yellow pulp. This type is eaten fresh and is also dried and sold as banana flakes. *Musa paradisiaca* grows from six to 12 inches long. It contains more starch and less sugar than the other kind. It is also called the plantain or red banana. This type is eaten cooked by the people who grow it. It is hardly ever exported.

The nutritional value of the banana is high. One banana is equal in value to two slices of bread, two ears of sweet corn, or one potato. It is a food that gives quick energy and is a good source of vitamins A, B, C, and G.

Bananas are easily and rapidly digested. Old people who are sick and babies who have not yet developed teeth can safely eat them. The peel makes the fruit easy to handle and ship, since no wrapping is necessary.

Banana plants are practical to grow for several reasons. They are not attacked by birds or insects until the fruit is ripe, and then it is ready to be picked, anyway. The plants will grow in any climate where the temperature does not fall below 50 degrees. In humid, tropical countries where the growing conditions are just right, 300 plants can be grown on one acre of ground. The soil needs to be deep, loose, and well drained to grow the best bananas. No weeding is necessary. The dense shade of the plant controls weed growth.

The people of the Philippines use banana leaves of the *Musa textilis* to make a tough rope. They also make a fiber from this plant that is strong enough to be woven into cloth. In countries where paper is expensive, the leaves of the banana plant are used for wrapping purposes. Many African huts are thatched with banana leaves. From a distance, an African village often looks like many stacks of banana leaves.

The United States imports more bananas than any other country. Most of the bananas imported to the West Coast come from the Pacific islands. On the East Coast, they come from Central and South America. The next largest users of bananas are Great Britain and France. South America exports more bananas than any other continent.

The banana plant is used in several ways.

thatch for houses

rope

banana flakes

fiber cloth

Man's Skin

Man's skin is called epithelial tissue. This kind of tissue lines every cavity and covers every surface of the body that might come into contact with foreign substances. For example, it lines parts of the nostrils, and lines and covers the uterus, the urinary bladder, the intestinal tract, the lungs, glands, and nerves.

Skin is a complicated organ, and it is our largest organ. If the surface of a man's skin were flat, it would cover nearly 20 square feet. It weighs about six pounds. It is a strong, soft, and flexible protective covering. If skin were stiff you could not bend your head, arms, or legs. But since it is elastic, it stretches and contracts to follow the movements of muscles and bones. The thickness of skin varies on different parts of the body. On the eyelids it is very thin—less than four one-hundredths of an inch. It is more than four times as thick on the palms of the hands and the soles of the feet.

Skin is made up of many layers of cells. The outer layers of epithelial cells are the epidermis. Skin is always exposed to wear and tear, and cold and heat. It is constantly being worn off and renewed. The outer cells of the epidermis—10 to 20 layers of them—are dead and dry. These cells flake off and new cells, produced in lower layers of the epidermis, push toward the surface. Fingernails are closely packed dead epithelial cells which are constantly being pushed out. There are no blood vessels found in the epidermis.

Under the epidermis is a part of the skin called the dermis. It connects with the epider-

mis above it, and with the fatty and connective tissue under it. The skin's blood vessels and nerves are in the dermis. The nerves send messages of touch and pain, as well as heat and cold to the brain. They protect the body by giving warning of injuries such as bruises and burns. In the dermis of the face and neck there are muscles whose movements make us smile or frown or move the surfaces of our faces. There are also muscles in the dermis attached to the hair follicles—the little hollows which contain hair roots. When these muscles contract, hairs rise and goose flesh occurs.

Connected with each hair follicle is a gland called a sebaceous gland. It secrets an oil onto the surface of the skin. This oily film helps keep skin pliable by keeping the water in it from drying up. The oil of the sebaceous glands also helps protect skin against infection.

Skin also contains sweat glands. The lower part of a sweat gland is in the dermis or just beneath it. A tiny tube extends from the gland to an opening in the surface of the skin called a pore. Sweat is a watery substance containing salt and other chemicals. It is one way in which we get rid of some of our body wastes. But a

Skin is elastic so it is able to follow the movements of muscles and bones.

Skin is thicker on the palms and soles. Calluses may form on the parts most exposed to wear.

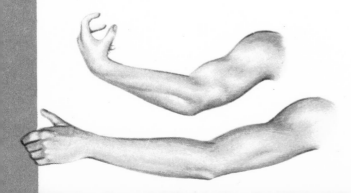

In this magnified section of skin the epidermis is shown by numbers (1) to (5). The dermis is shown by numbers (6) to (11). (1) The top layer is formed by flattened cells. The surface layers are dry and dead, and they flake off. (2) The second layer contains a fatty substance. This layer of the epidermis helps to keep the skin from losing water and salt. (3) The third layer is two to four cells thick. The cells become flattened in this layer. (4) The fourth, or prickle-cell layer, is several cells thick and the cells have an irregular shape. New cells are produced in the lower part of this layer and in the basal-cell layer below it. (5) In the basal-cell layer, the cells multiply continuously, and push the older layers towards the surface. (6) blood vessels (7) nerves (8) sweat gland, which produces sweat (9) pore, the opening through which the sweat comes out (10) sebaceous gland, which secretes an oily substance (11) hair follicle and hair

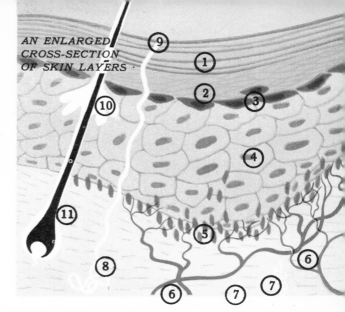

AN ENLARGED CROSS-SECTION OF SKIN LAYERS

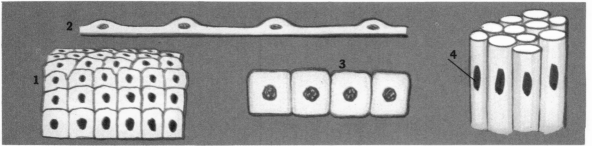

There are several kinds of epithelial cells. (1) Stratified epithelial tissue is made up of cells arranged in several layers. They are found in the skin and the mouth, among other places. The surface cells are flattened, the middle layer is cells of irregular shape, and the lowest layer is cubical cells of columnar cells. (2) Flattened epithelial cells are very thin, irregularly shaped cells. They cover the lungs and parts of the kidneys. They are also the surface cells of stratified epithelial tissue. (3) Cubical epithelial cells are found in certain glands and part of the brain. (4) Columnar epithelial cells cover the intestinal tract.

more important function of sweat is to cool the body. Heat causes us to sweat and the evaporation of sweat into the air cools the surface of our bodies.

Another function of skin is to produce Vitamin D. When sun shines on uncovered skin, Vitamin D is made. Vitamin D is particularly important in growing bodies for helping to form strong bones. Lack of it can cause rickets, a condition in which bones are soft and weak.

The color of skin—or pigmentation—is inherited. It is caused by three pigments—melanin which is brown, carotene which is yellow, and hemoglobin which is the red coloring in blood. Melanin is the main cause of the difference in skin colors of the various races. It is also what causes tanning when skin is exposed to rays of the sun. It is produced in special cells in the epidermis.

By looking at the back of a hand through a magnifying glass, you can see small intersecting lines and tiny pores on the surface of your skin.

Rodents, Hares, and Rabbits

There are few animals in the world as greedy as the enormous group known as rodents. These creatures are always gnawing at something. They gnaw at the bark of trees, at fruit and nuts, and at crops that have been planted by men. There are 6,400 different kinds of rodents, not including rabbits and hares, which are not true rodents.

The rodent has another reason for gnawing besides getting its food. It gnaws to wear down its front teeth. These teeth, called incisors, are curved. They grow throughout the rodent's life. If the animal did not keep them whittled down, they would eventually turn back and pierce its palate. Then the rodent would die.

The incisors are protected by enamel only on the front surfaces. So the teeth wear away faster at the back, keeping a constantly sharp cutting edge. Most rodents have two upper incisors and two lower ones. But rabbits and hares have an additional pair of upper incisors.

Rodents live in all parts of the world. Even in New Zealand, which is called the land without mammals, there are a few native rodents. Because rodents eat crops and are often dis-

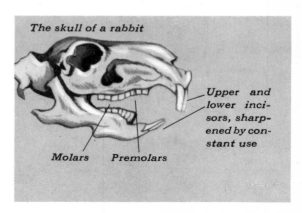

The skull of a rabbit

Molars   Premolars

Upper and lower incisors, sharpened by constant use

ease carriers, men hunt them and trap them.
(1) The dormouse is a tiny six-inch animal with five inches of tail. It lives in the woods of Europe and usually moves about only at night. It has the reputation of being sleepy because it hibernates longer than other animals.

(2) Hares may be two feet long with a three-inch tail. They are found practically all over the world, except in Australia. They sleep in hollows during the day, coming out at night for food. Hares move in jumps. They can cover 13 feet in one jump, and can reach a speed of 45 miles an hour.

1   2   3

(3) Porcupines live in North and South America, southern Europe, Africa, and many parts of Asia. The North American kinds are about three feet long. A porcupine's body is covered with hard hairs and strong, barbed quills which are sometimes 12 inches long.

(4) The capybara—the largest of the rodents—grows to more than four feet in length and almost two feet in height. It sometimes weighs more than 100 pounds. Capybaras are common in South America, where they live in dense forests near streams. They are timid, gentle animals, and are easily tamed.

(5) The wild rabbit may be almost a foot and a half long, with two inches of tail. They are found in many parts of the world, particularly in Australia. There they destroy so much growing food that 20,000,000 are killed every year.

(6) Coypu, big strong swimmers, may grow to be 20 inches long with 12-inch tails. They are natives of the rivers and streams of South America, but are now raised for their fur in many other parts of the world, too.

(7) Squirrels are familiar to nearly everyone with their long, bushy tails and quick movements. The squirrel shown here is a European pine squirrel, but there are hundreds of kinds of squirrels all over the world.

(8) The mouse and rat vary in size from the tiny pocket mouse, which weighs one third of

an ounce, to the African Giant rat with its 18-inch body and 18-inch tail. Rats and mice are killed by man everywhere because they damage crops and often carry serious diseases.

(9) Beavers are large rodents, almost three feet long with 12-inch tails. They are widespread in North America, Europe, and Asia. They live along streams and build their lodges with entrances under water.

(10) The chinchilla is about 10 inches long, with a six-inch tail. They inhabit the rocks and cliffs of the Andes Mountains in South America and are valued for their very costly fur. Chinchilla hair is so fine that a single strand cannot be seen without a magnifying glass.

(11) The prairie dog is a native of the North American prairies. It grows about a foot long, with four inches of tail. Prairie dogs live together in groups, in deep burrows which they dig out for themselves.

(12) Woodchucks or marmots are about two feet long with eight-inch tails. They live in Europe and America, eating enormously during the summer and hibernating during the winter.

(13) The guinea pig may be 10 inches long. Originally natives of Peru, where the Indians raised them for food, they are now raised in almost every part of the world. They are used in laboratories for experimental purposes, and are also grown for their fur.

10

13

12

11

Uruguay

Uruguay is the smallest independent nation in South America. It is wedged between two larger neighbors, Brazil on the north and east and Argentina on the west.

Uruguay was once part of Brazil and is quite similar geographically. It is a continuation of the Humid Pampa of Argentina, broken by ridges of the Brazilian Highland. Most of Uruguay's low hills, called *cuchillas*, are less than 500 feet above sea level, though one ridge, the Grande Principal, rises to nearly 1,600 feet.

The climate of Uruguay is temperate, neither very hot nor very cold. There is usually has more ranch animals in proportion to its population than any other country in the world. The animals are raised on huge ranches called *estancias*. Some of these are now being divided into many smaller, one-family ranches. Animals and animal products are Uruguay's biggest business and the basis for the country's wealth. Meat and meat products, wool, leather, and hides make up 95 percent of all goods exported from Uruguay. These goods are shipped to countries all over the world.

Although ranching is more important, there is considerable farming in Uruguay. The main

Panoramic view of the port of Montevideo. About one third of the population of Uruguay lives in Montevideo, which is Uruguay's capital city.

enough rainfall all year long, although droughts occasionally occur. Because of its gentle sloping hills, good climate, and plentiful supply of water, Uruguay is a good place to raise animals and crops. Animals there do not need cold weather shelters and can graze the year around on Uruguay's abundant and nourishing natural grasses.

About 60 percent of Uruguay's land is used for raising cattle and sheep. In fact, Uruguay crops are wheat, corn, linseed, sunflower seed, oats, barley, and rice. Wheat is planted on about half of Uruguay's farm land. Linseed is Uruguay's largest farm export.

Manufacturing is not yet very important in Uruguay, but it is being developed. Some of the products are textiles, leather goods, paper, plastics, cement, and tires of Brazilian rubber. Uruguay imports many manufactured goods, such as machinery and automobiles.

More than half of Uruguay's land is used for (1) raising cattle. Other land is used for (2) mixed farms and ranches, (3) farming, and (4) other uses.

More than a third of Uruguay's population lives in the capital and largest city, Montevideo. It is said that Montevideo got its name from a sailor with Magellan's expedition who saw a hill near the site of the present city and said "Monte vide eu," which is Portuguese for "I see a mountain." Montevideo is the eighth largest city in South America and a very popular resort for visitors from all over the world. It has an excellent natural harbor at which export and import goods are shipped to and received from all parts of the world.

There are two other important cities in Uruguay. They are Salto and Paysandu. Salto is located about 300 miles up the Uruguay River from Montevideo. Its port can be reached

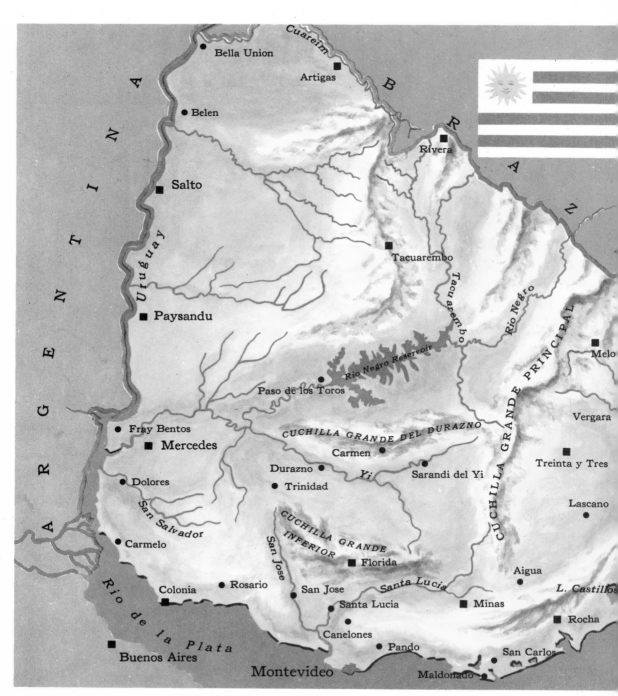

by ocean-going steamers. It is the railroad and meat packing center of Uruguay. Paysandu is on the Uruguay River between Salto and Montevideo and is also a port.

Before the first white men came from Europe, Uruguay's land was occupied by the Charrua Indians. These Indians fought the Europeans for many years. As a result, Uruguay was not settled by European colonists until long after settlers were established in Argentina and Brazil. Later, in 1828, after a war between Argentina and Brazil, Uruguay became an independent republic.

Uruguay is one of the most forward looking of the South American nations. It has a democratic government, and its laws are very progressive. The law provides that all adults in Uruguay have the right to vote.

All children in Uruguay must go to elementary school. High schools and colleges are free. All citizens are protected under hospital and medical care programs. Pensions are provided for old people. Uruguay is one of the few countries in the world where there is a minimum wage law with provisions that cover agricultural workers.

Uruguay's industries, including the railroads, are owned by the government. These industries make their products available to everyone at reasonable prices.

Most Uruguay homes have electricity, gas, and telephones. Uruguay has a strong economy as well as a progressive government, and the people enjoy a high standard of living.

Among the industrial and agricultural products of Uruguay are (1) *tires* (2) *leather and hides* (3) *wheat* (4) *linseed* (5) *rice* (6) *vegetables and fruits* (7) *sunflowers* (8) *tobacco.*

URUGUAY
AREA: *72,172 square miles*
POP: *2,700,000*
CAPITAL: *Montevideo City*
RELIGION: *Roman Catholic*
LANGUAGE: *Spanish*
MONETARY UNIT: *Peso (65.8¢)*

Scale of Miles
0   25   50

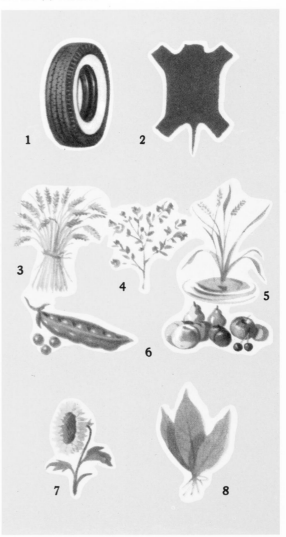

The Byzantine Empire

In the year A.D. 330 the Emperor Constantine moved the capital of the Roman Empire from Rome to the eastern city of Byzantium. Byzantium, which we know as Istanbul, was located on the Bosporus where Europe and Asia meet. From this location two great seas can be reached easily. They are the Mediterranean and the Black seas. Constantine chose Byzantium because it was an easier city to defend against the barbarian invaders from the east. The city could be attacked only by land from the west. Anyone who wished to attack Byzantium from the other sides would need a fleet of ships. The barbarian tribes of the north had no military fleets, so it was necessary to protect Byzantium only on the western side.

When Constantine decided to make Byzantium his eastern capital the city was already nearly 1,000 years old. It had been founded in the year 638 B.C. by Greek colonists. The city was named for Byzas, the leader of the colonists. When Constantine took the city he renamed it, in his honor, Constantinople.

Constantine gained fame for other reasons besides moving the capital of the Empire. He is remembered for making Christianity a lawful religion which it had not been until this time. And at the Battle of the Milvian Bridge in 312, Constantine is said to have won a great victory by using the sign of the cross with the *Monogram of Christ* as his battle flag. Constantine and the emperor who followed were thought of as picked by God, and it was the emperor's responsibility to direct the government, care for his people, and protect the church.

Another great event in the history of Byzantium occurred in A.D. 395, when the Emperor Theodosius divided the huge Empire into two parts, the Western Empire and the Eastern Empire. Constantinople became the capital of the eastern half of the Empire. From that time onwards the two empires had separate histories. The Western Empire fell to the barbarians in the year A.D. 476. The Eastern, or Byzantine, Empire lasted for another 1,000 years.

The greatest period in the history of the Byzantine Empire was during the reign of Emperor Justinian the Great, from A.D. 527 to 565.

An ambitious and wise man, Justinian had two aims in mind when he became emperor. He wished to restore the greatness of the old Roman Empire by conquering the lands held by

The Byzantines tried as much as possible to make Constantinople look like a Roman city, as in the above picture. In the background is the Cathedral of St. Sophia.

the barbarians. And, secondly, he wished to revise the old Roman law.

He succeeded in freeing North Africa from the Vandals, a barbarian tribe, and in chasing the Visigoths from Spain. But the conquest of Italy took a long time. In A.D. 555, after 20 years of fighting, Justinian and his army finally managed to drive the Goths out. Italy became a province of the Byzantine Empire and was governed by a Byzantine official. By the end of Justinian's reign, his empire stretched from the Strait of Gibraltar in the west, to the Euphrates River in the east.

Justinian gathered together all the Roman laws, from the earliest, which were written on 12 bronze tablets in 450 B.C., to those of Emperor Hadrian in A.D. 138. Twelve scholars were chosen to revise the laws and to fit them to the Christian religion. This enormous work took five years, but Justinian's Codex of Laws is still studied in modern law schools. His laws were much more humane than the Roman laws. For example, in the old Roman days, a thief was likely to be killed for his crime. During Justinian's reign he had only to pay four times the value of the stolen article.

The Byzantines did not invent a new architecture. Instead they took something from Roman, Greek, and Eastern styles, and combined them into their own architecture. Now called the Byzantine style, the most outstanding ex-

The old walls of Byzantium built by Emperor Theodosius in the fourth century

Roman Empire
Byzantine Empire

The top map shows the old Roman Empire and the Byzantine Empire. The bottom map shows the Byzantine Empire at the time of Justinian.

Byzantine Empire

Emperor Justinian the Great ruled the Byzantine Empire from A.D. 527 to 565. He revised the Roman code of laws to make it more just and humane.

ample of this architecture is the Cathedral of St. Sophia, which was begun for Justinian about A.D. 532. It is said that more than 10,000 men worked for six years to build this church. It was designed in the shape of a Greek cross. It had four aisles of equal length and a great dome in the center. The pillars, taken from old Asian temples, were of glowing purple, red, green, and white marble. The floor was decorated with rich mosaics, designs made by fitting together small pieces of colored materials.

A picture of Emperor Justinian done in mosaics in the Church of St. Vitale at Ravenna. During the fifth and sixth centuries Ravenna became the Western center for Byzantine mosaic.

The interior of the Cathedral of St. Sophia

The central aisle in the Church of St. Apollinare in Ravenna

During Justinian's reign, Constantinople became the most important commercial city in the world. The markets were full of carpets from Persia, jewels from India, silk from China, and wool from Spain. The emperor was anxious that the city should look like Rome, and many of the public buildings were of Roman design. For example, the Hippodrome, where chariot races and fights were held, was modeled after a Roman building.

After Justinian's death in A.D. 565 his empire fell to pieces. Most of Italy was lost to the Lombards. The Avars and Slavs came down from the lands near the Danube River toward the Adriatic Sea and settled in central Europe in what is now the country of Yugoslavia.

A long line of weak emperors followed Justinian. They had no sympathy for the poverty of their people and allowed their empire to fall into a decline.

During the Crusades, Constantinople was occupied for a short time by Baldwin of Flanders, who had himself elected Emperor. He treated the inhabitants with terrible cruelty. He and his men destroyed many of the beautiful art treasures gathered by Constantine and his successors. Beautiful bronze statues were melted down for metal coins.

In the last century of the Byzantine Empire, Constantinople was becoming more and more of a city-state rather than the capital of a great empire. The Ottoman Turks were approaching from the east. The Turkish crown prince crossed into Europe, and before long many western European towns and villages were in their hands. All the while they increased the size of their armies by forcing the conquered towns to give them the finest of their young men.

At last the Turks came upon the thick walls of Constantinople that had been built in the fourth century. These were really two walls 50 feet apart and fortified with towers every 150 feet or so.

The Emperor Constantine XI was in charge of the defenses of the city. When he knew Byzantium was lost to the enemy, he went to take the sacrament in the Cathedral of St. Sophia. Then he returned to defend the city. Be-

A mosaic which may be seen on a wall of the Church of Sant' Apollinare Nuovo in Ravenna. It represents the palace of King Theodoric.

fore long the besieging Turks trampled over his dead body on their way into the town. The streets were deserted, for the people had crowded into their great cathedral hoping for a last-minute miracle. But none came. And so, on May 29, 1453, Constantinople and the Byzantine Empire fell to the Turks. Sixty thousand women and children were sold into slavery.

After the conquest of Constantinople, most of the Greek students and scholars fled to Europe, carrying with them their manuscripts and documents. Thus the taking of Constantinople by the Turks had a tremendous effect on the course of history. For, with the flight of the scholars into Italy, a great new interest in learning spread over western Europe.

Magellan's Great Discovery

Ferdinand Magellan was a navigator and explorer who lived from about 1480 to 1521. He is famous for having been the leader of the first voyage around the world. Actually, he never completed the trip, as he was one of the many men who died before the long, difficult journey was over.

Magellan was Portuguese, but he made his main explorations on behalf of Spain. Spain's King Charles was most interested when Magellan proposed sailing across the Atlantic to find the Spice Islands, or Moluccas, by a western route. In return for a company of men and ships, Magellan agreed to claim all the land he found for Spain.

The Spanish king agreed, and gave Magellan what was needed for the voyage. In September, 1519, Magellan and his men sailed from the Spanish port of Sanlucar de Barrameda. He had five ships—the *Victoria*, the *Santiago*, the *Concepcion*, the *San Antonio*, and the flagship *Trinidad*, which Magellan commanded. The crew came from many parts of Europe. There were Spaniards, Portuguese, Italians, Frenchmen, Germans, Greeks, and English-

Contract between the King of Spain and Magellan

It is our will and a sign of our gratitude that we, in recognition of the exertions of this voyage, reward you by allowing you to keep a fifth of the net earnings that are obtained, after deducting the expenses of the fleet. In order that you may accomplish your plan we promise you five ships, two ships of 113 tons each and two of 90 tons, and one of 60 tons, with crews, supplies, and arms for two years. You will have 234 men including the captains, boatswains, and sailors.

This we promise and you have our royal word that we intend to protect you and will thus sign our name,

I, the King

Valladolid, 22 March 1518

men. Magellan even took a Malay slave he had got on an earlier journey to Malaya.

Three months after leaving Spain, the little fleet reached South America. It sailed into the bay of Rio de Janeiro to take on supplies and to repair damage to the ships. Magellan's ships left Rio in December, 1519, in search of a passage to the great ocean that lay to the west.

For three months the ships traveled down the coast of South America exploring every inlet and bay. By this time the southern winter was coming on and Magellan decided to remain on the east coast of South America in the bay of San Julian until spring. While Magellan's fleet was anchored at San Julian, the crews of three ships mutinied. Only the men of the *Santiago* and the *Trinidad* remained loyal. Fortunately, Magellan was able to quell the revolt, and he imprisoned the leaders.

Towards the end of May, the *Santiago* ventured forth to explore the seas to the south. The ship was wrecked, and the crew—when they

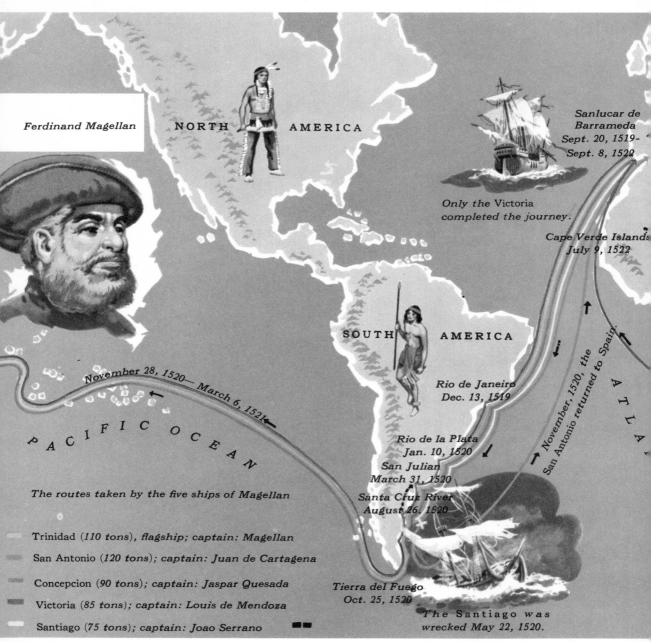

Ferdinand Magellan

NORTH AMERICA

Sanlucar de Barrameda
Sept. 20, 1519-
Sept. 8, 1522

Only the Victoria *completed the journey.*

Cape Verde Islands
July 9, 1522

November 28, 1520— March 6, 1521

SOUTH AMERICA

Rio de Janeiro
Dec. 13, 1519

PACIFIC OCEAN

November, 1520, the San Antonio returned to Spain.

ATLA

Rio de la Plata
Jan. 10, 1520

San Julian
March 31, 1520

Santa Cruz River
August 26, 1520

The routes taken by the five ships of Magellan

Trinidad (*110 tons*), *flagship; captain: Magellan*

San Antonio (*120 tons*); *captain: Juan de Cartagena*

Concepcion (*90 tons*); *captain: Jaspar Quesada*

Victoria (*85 tons*); *captain: Louis de Mendoza*

Santiago (*75 tons*); *captain: Joao Serrano*

Tierra del Fuego
Oct. 25, 1520

The Santiago was wrecked May 22, 1520.

finally were rescued by Magellan—were in bad condition. It was not until the end of August that the four remaining ships could set forth. Even then tremendous storms forced the ships to put in at the mouth of the Santa Cruz river.

While at Santa Cruz, Magellan began to have serious doubts as to whether there really was a passage through to the vast ocean west of South America. He had no idea that the very goal he was seeking lay only two days' sail away.

In October, 1520, behind a headland that jutted out into the sea, the expedition sighted a narrow strait. Magellan sent two ships to explore it. This time they came back with the long-awaited news. The strait did not grow narrower. Instead, it seemed to split the land in two.

The four ships sailed into the passage. The men were afraid. Not only was the weather very stormy, but the strait was bounded by steep, overhanging cliffs. At night these crags

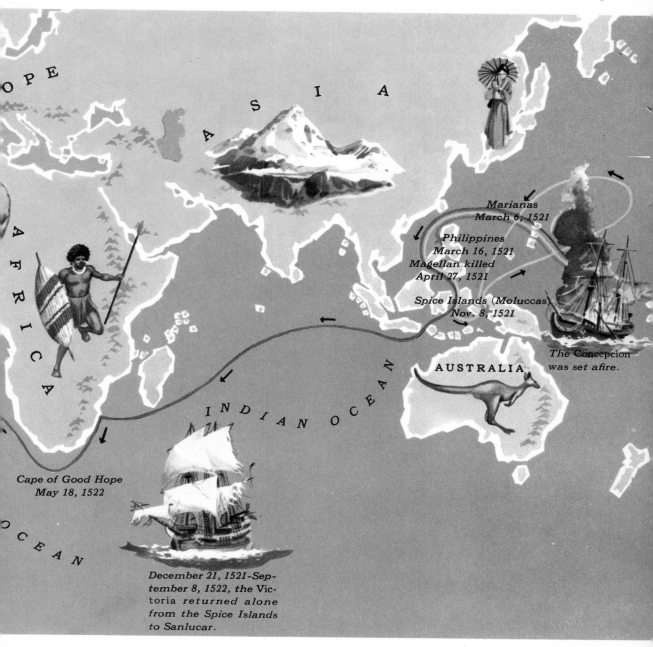

Marianas
March 6, 1521

Philippines
March 16, 1521
Magellan killed
April 27, 1521

Spice Islands (Moluccas)
Nov. 8, 1521

The Concepcion
was set afire.

AUSTRALIA

INDIAN OCEAN

Cape of Good Hope
May 18, 1522

December 21, 1521-September 8, 1522, the Victoria returned alone from the Spice Islands to Sanlucar.

were lit up by the dancing flames of Indian campfires. Magellan's men named the land Tierra del Fuego—Land of Fire.

The pilot of the *San Antonio* was fearful of this strange place. He managed to imprison his own captain and turn his ship back to Spain before Magellan realized what had happened.

On November 28, 1520, Magellan and his men reached the end of the strait, which is now called the Strait of Magellan. They came in sight of an endless ocean. The water was calm and the breezes were gentle. They had reached the Pacific Ocean, which means peaceable or calm. By this time most of the sailors' food was gone, because the main provisions had been on the *San Antonio*. For 98 days they sailed across the Pacific. Many of the crew died of scurvy. They had no water and were forced to hunt the ships' rats, to eat sawdust, and to chew leather in order just to keep alive.

Finally they arrived at the Ladrones, a group of islands now known as the Marianas. There they obtained some food and water before sailing on again. After several weeks they reached the Philippine Islands. The native chief on the island of Zebu welcomed the sailors. He told Magellan that he was at war with the neighboring island of Matan. Magellan promised to help and led his sailors in an attack. They were met by a tremendous number of warriors, and Magellan was killed. Magellan

died without knowing that one of his ships would be the first to sail around the world.

The Zebu chief turned upon the European sailors and killed many of them. Of the 260 men who originally set out from Spain, only 114 remained to man the three ships. They burned the most heavily damaged one, the *Concepcion*. The other two sailed on from island to island, but the men usually did not go ashore for fear of the natives.

At last they landed at the Spice Islands. They had come halfway around the world. The *Trinidad* and the *Victoria* loaded up with a precious cargo of spices and set out for home. They had not gone far, however, before the *Trinidad* sprang a leak and had to turn back.

So the *Victoria* continued alone. She went through the Indian Ocean, and, under the leadership of Sebastian del Cano, rounded the Cape of Good Hope. When they reached the Cape Verde Islands, some of the men were forced to land because of hunger and exhaustion. They were taken prisoner by the Portuguese, who did not wish to see the Spanish ship reach its destination. However, those left aboard continued their journey.

On September 8, 1522, they sailed into Sanlucar de Barrameda. This was the same port from which, three years earlier, they had headed west. This ended man's first trip around the world.

Magellan was killed while helping to fight a local battle on the island of Matan.

The Straits of Magellan were lit up at night by Indian campfires.

Thomas Jefferson

When the rebellion of the American colonies was a year old, the Continental Congress in Philadelphia decided it was time to notify the world that they were fighting for complete independence and that they intended to form a new nation.

One of the delegates to the Congress was 33-year-old Thomas Jefferson, a big-boned, lanky lawyer from the colony of Virginia. Because he had a talent for clear thinking and clear writing, he was asked to make a rough draft of a declaration of independence. Jefferson spent 17 days on the document, hunched over a portable writing desk. Minor changes were suggested by Benjamin Franklin, John Adams, and others.

With few changes, Jefferson's draft was accepted by the Congress on July 4, 1776. Ever since then the Fourth of July has been the greatest national holiday in the United States.

In the Declaration of Independence, Jefferson wrote that "all men are created equal." He believed this deeply and passionately. But it was a rather unusual belief for anybody with Jefferson's family background. His mother was a member of one of Virginia's wealthiest and most aristocratic families, the Randolphs. His father had been a large landowner.

Thomas Jefferson was 33 when he drafted the Declaration of Independence in 1776. Benjamin Franklin was one of the delegates who helped Jefferson revise the draft.

Jefferson's parents had settled in the frontier wilderness of Albemarle county, Virginia. He was born there in 1743, and later he went to William and Mary College in Williamsburg, the capital of the colony. He was a brilliant student, a fine athlete and horseman, and an accomplished musician. All this, plus his great personal charm, made him much in demand at social gatherings.

The estate that he had inherited from his father grew until it covered 5,000 acres of land. Jefferson could have led the life of a country gentleman, but after college he took up the study of law.

Then one day, when he was 22, he stood in the corridor of the House of Burgesses, Virginia's colonial legislature, and heard Patrick Henry make his famous demand, "Give me liberty or give me death." From then on, young Tom Jefferson was fired with the idea of taking part in the colonists' fight for their rights. He was elected to the House of Burgesses in 1769. In 1776, when the Revolution began, he was sent to represent Virginia in the Continental Congress. By this time, he had written a pamphlet on political rights that was widely read and quoted.

Jefferson was not cut out for soldiering. During the Revolutionary War he took no part in the fighting, but devoted himself mainly to the new government of Virginia, as a legislator and later as governor. He wanted Virginia's state laws to be progressive and democratic. He hoped they would serve as models for laws in other states.

Many of his ideas were accepted. For example, Virginia led the way in guaranteeing religious freedom, in public education, and in fairer inheritance laws. Jefferson also was against slavery, but Virginia refused to enact any of the anti-slavery measures he suggested.

Jefferson was 39 when his wife, Martha, died in 1782, leaving him a widower with two small daughters. Theirs had been a devoted marriage of 10 years, and griefstricken, Jefferson decided to retire from public life.

But he was far too important to the young nation to be allowed to retire, and he was called back into public service.

Re-elected to Congress, he created the monetary system that we use today. He succeeded Benjamin Franklin as minister to France, and traveled widely in Europe. He made friends everywhere for the infant republic which he represented.

He returned to the United States and had 10 bitter, stormy years as Secretary of State in Washington's cabinet and as Vice President during Adams' administration. It seemed to Jefferson that the new country was in danger of being run by a handful of wealthy, privileged men. He fought Adams and Alexander Hamilton for the kind of democracy that he believed in.

Thomas Jefferson designed and supervised the building of Monticello—little mountain—his home near Charlottesville, Virginia.

In 1803, President Jefferson bought over 800,000 square miles of western territory from France, doubling the size of the United States.

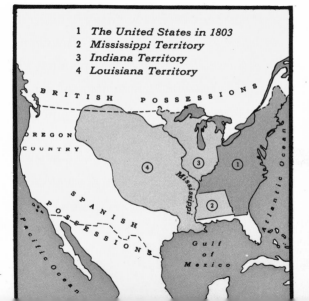

1 *The United States in 1803*
2 *Mississippi Territory*
3 *Indiana Territory*
4 *Louisiana Territory*

Flag raising ceremony in the Louisiana Territory

or entirely included in this huge new territory.

The same year, Jefferson showed his lively interest in the nation's future expansion by sending two explorers, Captain Merriwether Lewis and William Clark, on an exploration trip across the continent to the Pacific.

Jefferson was 66 when he retired to Monticello, the beautiful plantation home in Virginia which he had designed. He lived another 16 years, and he did so in ways that have made him a perfect example of the retired, cultivated gentleman. He showed curiosity about everything. He engaged in scientific farming. He corresponded with famous statesmen and scholars. He was host to distinguished visitors from all over the world.

Not far from his home, Jefferson founded the University of Virginia, attending to every detail personally. He was an accomplished architect and planned its buildings. He chose its faculty. Today, the University has one of the loveliest campuses in the country, a tribute to Jefferson's good taste.

Jefferson lived to be 83, and he died in 1826 on the day he helped to make famous—the 4th of July. He himself chose what was to be written on his tomb—what he considered his greatest accomplishments—"Here was buried Thomas Jefferson, Author of the Declaration of Independence, of The Statute of Virginia for Religious Freedom, and Father of the University of Virginia."

In 1800, John Adams and his Federalist party were swept out of power and Jefferson became third President of the United States.

He served two terms. One of his achievements was the Louisiana Purchase in 1803. For about 15,000,000 dollars, President Jefferson bought from France a tract of land that doubled the existing area of the United States. With the land went the port of New Orleans and free passage on the Mississippi River. Thirteen of the present 50 states were either partly

Lewis and Clark were sent by Jefferson on an expedition from 1803 to 1806 to explore the Louisiana Territory and the Pacific Northwest. With their Indian guides, they reached the Pacific Ocean in November, 1805, opening the way for future traders and settlers and establishing America's claim to that country.

Antarctica

Antarctica was the last continent to be discovered, and it is by far the unfriendliest to human life. In fact, it will probably never support any real civilization. Nevertheless, Antarctica is very important to the world.

The southern polar region is very different from the northern polar region, where there is only ice floating on the Arctic Ocean. At the South Pole there is a great continent, equal in size to Australia and Europe combined, and half again as large as the United States.

Antarctica is more isolated than any other continent. To reach it, ships or planes must cross 600 miles of deep ocean and be exposed to the fiercest winds in the world. North of Antarctica, between about 55 degrees and 65 degrees South latitude, there is a band of open ocean that runs all around the world. This is the home of the permanent west winds. It is the rugged gateway to Antarctica, and it is not surprising that no human being went south of it before the end of the 18th century.

The greater part of Antarctica is a plateau, marked by high and rugged mountains. The plateau averages about 8,000 feet above sea level, which is more than twice as high as the

Many nations have claimed parts of Antarctica. But the United States believes the continent should be internationally owned and governed.

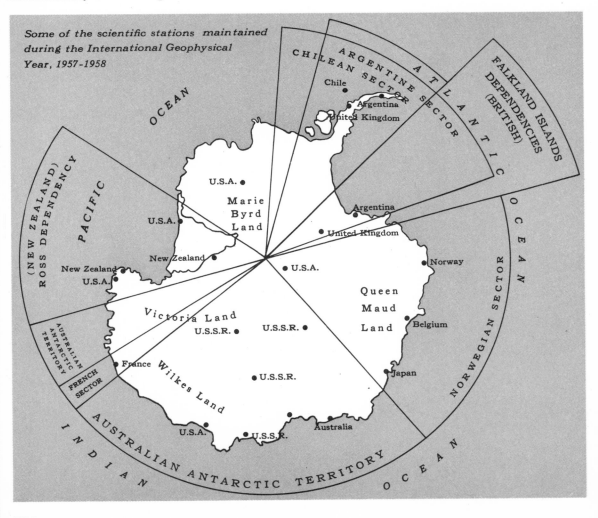

Some of the scientific stations maintained during the International Geophysical Year, 1957–1958

average height of Asia, the next highest continent. But Antarctic explorers must travel at higher elevations even than that, for the entire continent, except for small parts in summer, is covered by an immense sheet of ice that is from 1,000 to 14,000 feet thick. There is so much ice that if it all melted the world's oceans would rise 80 feet. This unlikely event would submerge most of the major cities on earth, since most of them are near the sea.

The great sheet of ice that covers Antarctica extends out into the sea on every side. This is especially true on the Pacific side, where the Ross Shelf Ice covers much of the Ross Sea. This great shelf of ice is roughly the size of France. It is from 500 to 1,000 feet thick, and it juts more than 400 miles out to sea. Since it floats on the ocean, most of it is beneath the surface. But it rises straight up from the water, sometimes as much as 200 feet. In summer large blocks of this ice break off and float northward until they disintegrate in the warmer water. These icebergs are sometimes as much as 90 miles long.

Beyond the shelf ice is sea ice, which builds up in winter and melts again in summer. But there is always some floating ice in Antarctic waters, and ships often need icebreaking equipment when they sail in these waters.

For convenience in studying Antarctica, geographers have divided the continent into four parts by drawing lines that cross each other at right angles at the South Pole. The parts are called the Weddell, Ross, Victoria, and Enderby quadrants. This division has little to do with political or geological realities. Many nations have claimed territory on the continent, and some of the claims conflict. The United States does not recognize any claims. It believes that the continent should be international.

Geologically, the continent is divided into two main parts. West Antarctica, about one third of the whole, is divided from East Antarctica by a deep depression that runs across the continent. Some of this depression is below sea level and it is possible that Antarctica is not one continent, but several large land masses with connecting seas.

The volcano Mt. Erebus is 13,200 feet high.

There are several mountain ranges in Antarctica. The largest of them curves southward from Cape North and touches the Ross Sea. It contains several high peaks, the highest of which is Mt. Markham at 15,100 feet. At the edge of the Ross Shelf Ice are twin volcanoes, Mt. Erebus and Mt. Terror. Mt. Erebus, 13,200 feet high, is still active and smoking.

Traces of minerals have been found in Antarctica, although none has yet been found that can be used commercially. There are very large low grade coal deposits. Coal found today could have been formed only in places where there

Ships often become blocked in the drifting pack ice of the polar seas.

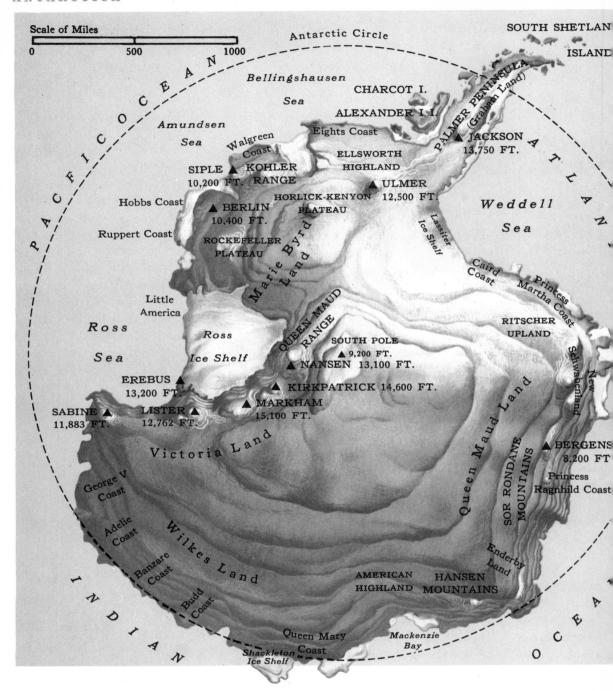

was once thick vegetation, which was buried and then subjected to immense pressure for thousands of years. Because coal is found in Antarctica, we know that the climate was once very different than it is today.

The climate at present is extremely cold. Temperatures have been recorded as low as 125 degrees below zero Fahrenheit. The average temperature, even in summer, does not rise above zero. Fierce winds howl across these bare wastes. The average wind velocity at several weather stations has been recorded as 50 miles an hour. Winds of 100 miles an hour are common. Not much snow falls each year—only about a foot a year on the coast, and less inland. What snow does fall, however, never melts, as the weather is too cold.

There are several manned weather stations in Antarctica, and there are a number of scien-

Huge icebergs are sometimes a danger to shipping.

tific expeditions presently learning about this newest of the earth's lands. But there is no permanent population. If men were to inhabit Antarctica, they would have to live without fresh vegetables, for there are none, and none can be grown. The only vegetation is a few mosses, lichens, and algae which grow in the short summers. However, there are many birds and animals, most of which live in the sea. The penguin is the typical and most famous native of Antarctica, but there are also several kinds of seals, whales, and other marine mammals, as well as many kinds of fish.

The first man to sail south of the Antarctic Circle for an extended period of time was Captain James Cook, the famous English explorer. In 1772 he led two ships on a tour of the Antarctic, and in 1774 he reached a latitude of 71 degrees 10 minutes south, the southernmost point attained in the 18th century. But he saw no land. He assumed that there was none, as at the North Pole where there was nothing but floating ice.

Soon after Cook returned, sealers and whalers began to explore the region. A Russian expedition under Admiral Fabian Gottlieb von Bellingshausen journeyed south, and in 1821 sighted the first land ever seen within the Antarctic Circle, the little island of Peter I.

Several English explorers, with the finan-

cial support of a British whaling firm, explored the area in the next few years. The Weddell Sea was named after one of them.

An American expedition under Charles Wilkes sailed south in 1839. Wilkes reported seeing land where later it could not be found. But he was the first man to state that a continent actually existed within the Polar Circle.

In the same year Captain James Clark Ross led a British expedition that made important discoveries and landed parties on Ross Shelf Ice. Ross first sighted the twin volcanoes on this shelf and named them after his two ships.

Norwegian, German, and English explorers surveyed the polar seas during the next 50 years. Around 1900 the pace of exploration quickened. Captain Robert Falcon Scott and Ernest Henry Shackleton, two English explorers, made their first journey southward, and Germans and Norwegians continued their work. In 1909, Shackleton went by hand drawn

The most famous inhabitant of Antarctica is the penguin. Fortunately for penguins, their skins are not valuable, and they are not hunted.

sledge to a latitude of 88 degrees 23 minutes South, within a short distance of the Pole, which is at 90 degrees South. Three years later, on December 14, 1911, Roald Amundsen, a Norwegian, reached the South Pole. A month later Scott and four companions also reached the Pole. Amundsen returned fairly easily, but Scott and his party were caught by a blizzard and perished in a tent only 10 miles from their supply depot.

There have been many expeditions since this famous tragedy. Notable are several trips made by Admiral Richard E. Byrd, of the

sound waves to return to them after bouncing off the ground below the ice. This told them how deep the ice was. It is the only practical way to survey most of Antarctica.

In the same year Vivian Fuchs, a British explorer, crossed the continent from the Weddell Sea to the Ross Sea, stopping at the Pole along the way. He took with him several caterpillar tractors especially adapted for travel on ice and snow. This is probably the Antarctic transportation of the future.

Today explorations continue. There are permanent American and Russian scientific

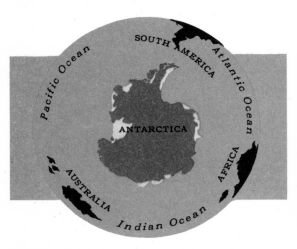

Relationship of the continent of Antarctica to surrounding continents.

A machine measures the height of the tides in the Antarctic Circle.

United States. Byrd made a number of flights over the Pole before World War II, established a base camp called Little America on the Ross Shelf Ice, and spent several months alone at a weather station more than 100 miles south of Little America. In 1946 Byrd led the largest of all Antarctic expeditions, called Operation Highjump. Byrd had under his command more than 4,000 men, 13 ships, many motor vehicles, and several airplanes. Aerial photographs were taken of much of the continent.

During the International Geophysical Year —1957-1958—scientists from 12 nations cooperated in the exploration of Antarctica.

In 1958 a team of five American scientists discovered a new mountain range near the Weddell Sea. They exploded charges in the ice and then measured the time it took for the

parties in Antarctica at the present time, and expeditions from other countries often undertake special projects. The secrets of the icebound continent are gradually being revealed to scientists. On December 1, 1959, the United States, the Soviet Union, the United Kingdom, France, Norway, Belgium, Australia, New Zealand, Argentina, Chile, Japan, and South Africa signed a treaty reserving Antarctica for peaceful uses.

It is doubtful that the South Pole will become a popular place to live because of the extremely cold climate and the absence of vegetation. However, for those who are working and studying there the continent presents the challenge of an unknown land—of which one third is still unexplored—and of living in ways which are unique on earth.

Nebuchadnezzar built the Processional Street, which was paved with slabs of limestone. He faced the walls with blue brick decorated with colorful enameled lions. At the New Year a statue of the god Marduk was carried down the street and through the Gate of Ishtar.

Nebuchadnezzar and the Wonders of Babylon

The modern country of Iraq was known thousands of years ago as Mesopotamia. Mesopotamia means the Land Between Two Rivers. In this country, bounded by the Tigris and Euphrates rivers, some of the earliest civilizations in the world reached their height. Just as Egypt was made fertile by the Nile, Mesopotamia was made fertile by its rivers, and its people had a richer life than those of other nations.

One of the richest of these civilizations belonged to the Babylonians. Their empire lasted through two different periods. It began about 2,000 years before the birth of Christ, and by 1700 B.C., one of Babylon's great kings, Hammurabi, had laid down a famous code of laws for his kingdom.

After Hammurabi's death Babylon was attacked by various tribes, and finally the Assyri-

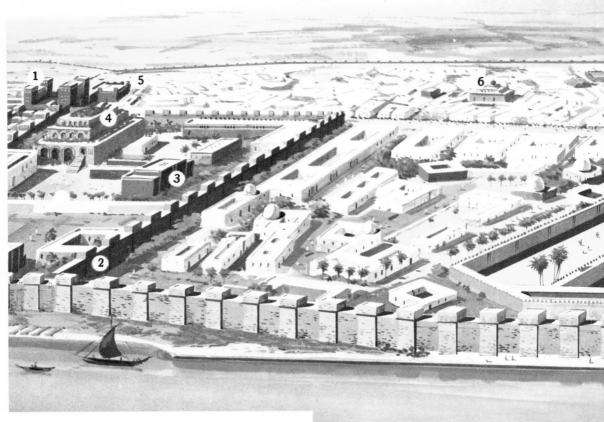

KEY TO THE WONDERS OF BABYLON

(1) *Gate of Ishtar* (2) *walls outside the royal palace*
(3) *throne room* (4) *Hanging Gardens* (5) *Temple of Ninmak* (6) *Temple of Ishtar* (7) *market*
(8) *Tower of Babel* (9) *Temple of Marduk* (10) *brick bridge over the Euphrates*

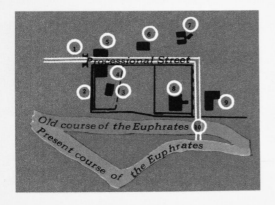

In ancient times the Euphrates River followed a different course, passing right through the city.

Nebuchadnezzar rebuilt the ancient city of Babylon.

ans, on the other side of the Tigris, conquered the whole of Mesopotamia. They ruled until 612 B.C., when the Chaldeans from southeastern Mesopotamia rose under the rule of General Nabopolassar. Assisted by the Medes, from the ancient kingdom of Media, they took Babylon and completely defeated the Assyrian armies. Nabopolassar made himself king of Babylon, and he and his son Nebuchadnezzar began immediately to rebuild the great city.

When Nabopolassar died, the new king, Nebuchadnezzar, continued his father's efforts to make the Babylonian Empire as great as it

He added a third wall to the city and made the Tower of Babel into a shrine to his god Marduk.

once had been. Even before his father's death, Nebuchadnezzar had led the Babylonian armies against Pharaoh Necho of Egypt, whose armies had invaded Syria and Judah, the kingdom which is modern Palestine. In a great Babylonian victory, Necho's army was defeated and driven out of Syria and Judah, leaving the Babylonians in control.

It was at this time that Nebuchadnezzar learned of his father's death and returned to take the Babylonian crown. For a time Nebuchadnezzar had affairs of state to occupy him. But he was still expanding his empire. During the seventh year of his reign the people of Phoenicia rebelled. He conquered its chief city, Tyre.

In 597 the state of Judah under King Jehoiachim revolted against the Babylonians, and Nebuchadnezzar sent his army into Judah. They captured the young King Jehoiachim and his family and brought them as captives to Babylon. In his place they set up King Zedekiah to rule Judah.

Nine years later, with the help of a new Egyptian Pharaoh, Zedekiah and the people of Judah rebelled once more against the Babylonians. But when Nebuchadnezzar sent his

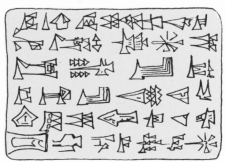

Nebuchadnezzar's seal was stamped on all the bricks used in his rebuilding of Babylon.

powerful army against them, the Egyptians retreated and the Jews were left to defend Jerusalem alone. After 18 months, the city was captured and destroyed, and a great many of the Jewish people were taken into Babylon as captives. This is described as the Babylonian Captivity.

We know from the Bible that Nebuchadnezzar was a proud and ruthless man. He had a golden statue of his god, Marduk, set up, and those who refused to worship it were thrown into a blazing furnace. The Bible also tells of Nebuchadnezzar's madness. In the last years of his life he crawled on his hands and knees outside the city, eating grass like an animal. He died in 562 B.C. His successors were weak men. A little more than 20 years later the Babylonian Empire was conquered by Cyrus of Persia.

Portrait of King Nebuchadnezzar, carved in stone

Although Babylon had been built more than 1,000 years before his time, Nebuchadnezzar did much to rebuild it and to add to its glories. First, as was fitting for a warrior-king, he built a great third wall to the east of the city. He described it in his own words: "I caused a mighty wall to circumscribe Babylon in the east. I dug its moat; and its battlements I built out of asphalt and fired bricks. I gave it wide gates and set in doors of cedar wood sheathed with copper. I surrounded them with mighty floods. In order that no one might break through by way of the moat, I heaped up a heap of earth beside it and surrounded it with walls of brick."

Modern excavations have found that Nebuchadnezzar's boast was not exaggerated. There were indeed three walls of brick, the thickest of which was 25 feet wide.

Another famous building at Babylon was the Tower of Babel. This great pyramidlike temple was built long before Nebuchadnezzar's time, but it had been allowed to decay. Now Nebuchadnezzar pledged himself to raise up the top of the temple so that it would "rival heaven." The Tower of Babel was built in seven steps, each one smaller than the one below it. The base of the tower was 288 feet square, and the tower was 288 feet high. Some 58,000,000 bricks went into the making of it. At the top of the tower was a shrine to the Babylonian god, Marduk. This was plated with gold and bluish enamel work which glittered brilliantly and could be seen for many miles.

The lower temple had a golden statue of the god, which could be visited by pilgrims. The Greek historian, Herodotus, who came to Babylon 150 years later, saw this statue of pure gold and estimated that it weighed about 26 tons. The pilgrims could visit the statue by marching up the outside of the tower to this lower temple. Only the priests could visit the shrine of Marduk, which they reached by climbing an inner, secret stair to the top.

Another wonder of ancient Babylon was the famous Hanging Gardens, although Nebuchadnezzar did not build them. They were supposed to have been built years before for Queen Semiramis, who longed for the cool gardens of

Leaving Jerusalem in flames behind them, the Jews were carried off as captives by the Babylonian army, which fought for Nebuchadnezzar.

her native Media. There is no record that Semiramis ever lived, but the ruins of gardens have been found. Archways built over a well showed how water was pumped up to irrigate the trees and plants on the roof of the palace. In ancient days, these gardens were considered one of the seven wonders of the world.

One of Nebuchadnezzar's greatest accomplishments was the processional street which he built. The street ran from the outer city walls to the gate of the goddess Ishtar. It was paved with limestone slabs, and its walls were faced with glazed blue brick. As many as 120 brightly enameled lions spaced 64 feet apart ornamented the walls. The lions were gaily colored in white, yellow, and red. Nebuchadnezzar wrote of this feat himself, saying, "I made the way a shining one." So that there be no doubt that Nebuchadnezzar built it, every paving block along the way was inscribed: "Nebuchad-

755

nezzar, King of Babylon, am I. The Babel Street I paved with slabs for the procession of the great lord Marduk." And the paving slabs were laid face down so that the inscriptions would be preserved.

This Processional Street served another purpose as well. Nebuchadnezzar, always the warrior, had designed the street for the defense of the city. It was nearly 74 feet wide and straight, with 22-foot walls on either side of it. Anyone wishing to attack the palace would have to make his way through this street, and so he would easily be trapped within the walls.

In spite of this cleverly planned street, and his strong walls, Nebuchadnezzar's empire fell soon after he died. The walls never were destroyed, but the people within surrendered. Years later, Babylon became a desert, its great ruins buried under the sand. As the prophet Jeremiah prophesied in the Bible: "None shall remain in it, neither man nor beast . . . it shall be desolate forever."

One of the 120 lions which decorated the walls of the Processional Street

The Hanging Gardens of Babylon was considered one of the seven wonders of the ancient world.

A rocket blasts off the launching pad. In its nose is a satellite that will be ejected from the rocket in space and placed in orbit.

An artificial satellite circles the earth, radioing information back to the ground by means of its antennae.

Satellites in the Space Age

The space age began in 1957, when the Soviet Union launched *Sputnik I*—the first satellite put into orbit by man. Today such launchings are commonplace. Hardly a month goes by without the newspapers carrying the story of another satellite launching from Cape Canaveral or Vandenberg Air Force Base in the United States, or from the Soviet Union. American and Russian scientists are putting new satellites into orbit around the earth with increasing regularity and reliability.

Each satellite has a definite scientific function. Some measure the radiation belts through which man must travel if he is to reach other planets. Some send animals, such as mice, dogs, or monkeys, far out into space to test the effect of weightlessness upon the body. Others are used for purposes of communication by reflecting radio waves over great distances. And still others are used to take pictures of the land or weather below.

In the fall of 1960, there were more than 35 objects circling the earth. Fewer than half of them are satellites. The rest are called space garbage and are various stages of the rockets used to launch the satellites. When these rocket parts are released, they also go into orbit. The satellites are exploring the regions of space where man will travel some day.

Until about five years ago, most scientists would have defined a satellite as a small planet revolving around a larger one. The planet Saturn, for instance, has 9 satellites. The earth has one natural satellite—the moon.

The laws that govern the motion of planets also govern the motion of the man-made satellites. The laws of motion of the planets were known in Isaac Newton's time, almost 300 years ago. But they could not be usefully applied to the orbiting of an artificial satellite until the modern technologies of electronics and rocketry were developed.

Any object within the earth's gravitational influence will be attracted to the earth. A baseball thrown up in the air will return to earth. The faster you throw it away from you, the higher it will rise, and the longer it will take to return. But it will always return—unless you throw it so hard that it can escape from the earth's gravity entirely and travel into outer space. You would have to throw the ball at a speed of over 25,000 miles an hour for this to happen. If a rocket achieves this speed, it will leave the earth entirely and never return.

The rocket will not be free, however, although it has escaped the earth's gravity. Like the earth itself, the rocket will be affected by the sun's gravity. It will go into orbit around the sun. Space probes such as *Pioneer IV* have become satellites of the sun, orbiting just as the planets in the solar system do. *Pioneer IV* will

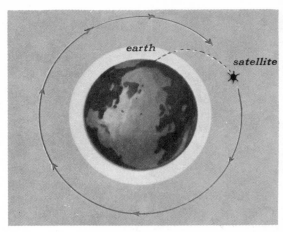

An artificial satellite, having reached a velocity of about 16,000 miles per hour, travels around the earth in its own orbit, which is not actually parallel to the earth's surface, but elliptical.

A bucket of water can be swung over a man's head without any water being spilled. Centrifugal force, shown by the red arrow, keeps the water pressed against the bottom of the bucket.

When a baseball is thrown into the air, the earth's gravity pulls it back, as if the earth were a magnet.

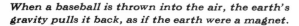

never return to the earth—but it will never leave the solar system.

A satellite that orbits the earth is caught in the earth's gravity, like the baseball. But, unlike the baseball, it does not fall back to the ground. This is because of centrifugal force. Centrifugal force is the force that makes a body moving in a curved path tend to pull away from the center of the circle of which the path is a part. If you slowly swing a bucket full of water at the end of your arm and over your head, you would probably get wet. The force of gravity would cause the water to tumble down on you. But if you swing the bucket

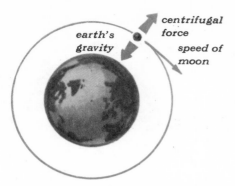

The moon is attracted by the earth's gravity, but the speed of the moon in its orbit creates a centrifugal force that balances the earth's pull. As a result, the moon maintains its orbit.

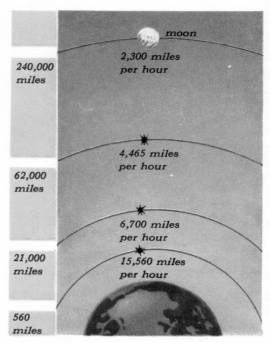

The farther a satellite is from the earth, the slowe. the rate at which it travels.

faster, so that it keeps turning above your head, the water will not spill out, even when the bucket is directly upside down.

Centrifugal force presses the water against the bottom of the bucket. The speed of rotation determines how strong that force is. If you swing the bucket slowly, the centrifugal force will be weaker than the pull of gravity—too weak to hold the water in the bucket. If you swing the bucket too fast, the centrifugal force will become so strong that it may tear the bucket out of your hand, and the water and bucket will both go sailing away from you.

Centrifugal force keeps satellites in orbit. There is no human arm to keep the satellite traveling around the earth, but there is an invisible arm—the force of gravity. If the satellite travels too fast—over 25,000 miles per hour— that arm will lose its grip. The force of gravity will be overcome by centrifugal force, and the satellite, like the bucket, will fly away from the center—the earth. If the satellite travels too slowly in its orbit, gravity will be stronger than centrifugal force, and the satellite will fall back to earth—like the water in the bucket.

The centrifugal force needed to keep a satellite in orbit depends upon the force of gravity of the planet, and upon the satellite's distance from the planet. The farther away a satellite is from the earth, the weaker the force of gravity is, and the slower the satellite's speed has to be. This is true of all satellites, whether natural or man-made.

The moon, which is about 240,000 miles

from the earth, travels about the earth once every 27 1/3 days. This comparatively slow rate of travel keeps it in its orbit. But the moon is gradually moving farther away from the earth. By the year A.D. 50,000,000, it will be about 340,000 miles away and it will take 47 days to travel once around the earth.

A man-made satellite, on the other hand, usually travels just above the earth's atmosphere. It must travel at this height or the friction of the air will burn it up. At a distance of 175 miles from the surface a satellite orbits the earth every hour and a half at a speed of approximately 17,130 miles per hour.

The earth itself must maintain a certain speed as it travels around the sun—approximately 67,000 miles per hour. If it did not, it would be unable to stay in its present orbit.

Satellites, natural or man-made, obey the forces of gravity wherever they are. Where and how a satellite goes into orbit depends entirely upon its speed. Man can put satellites around the earth, the moon, and the sun. And he will undoubtedly place satellites in orbit around other planets in the solar system as his skills in probing space progress.

Catherine
the Great

Catherine II, one of the greatest rulers of the Russian Empire, had been born a poor and unknown German princess in Stettin, Prussia, in 1729. She was christened Sophia Augusta Frederica.

Although her family talked of making a good marriage for Sophia, she was considered plain and unattractive. She often thought she would remain unmarried like her many spinster aunts. But Empress Elizabeth of Russia, daughter of Peter the Great, had made her nephew Peter heir to the throne. She wished to find a wife for Peter, and selected Sophia, who was his distant cousin.

At the age of 15, Sophia Augusta and her mother, Princess Johanna Elizabeth, were brought to Moscow by carriage and sleigh to meet the young bridegroom. Empress Elizabeth greeted them and took an instant liking to Sophia. The Grand Duke Peter, who was also only 15, was less interested in his new bride. Peter was a weak boy with the mind of a child and an inability to learn anything. His life had been ruined by a brutal Swedish military man who had been his tutor. Peter cared only for military drills and toy soldiers.

The young couple were not to be married for a year. During that time Sophia became a close friend of Empress Elizabeth's. She was converted to the Russian Orthodox religion and was rechristened Catherine Alexeyevna. In 1745 she was married to Peter and became the Grand Duchess.

Their marriage was an unhappy one. Peter disliked Catherine and remained abnormally childish. Much to Elizabeth's disappointment, Catherine did not bear a child for 10 years. When a son, Paul, was finally born, the old Empress took charge of him completely. Catherine never showed any interest in her son.

In 1762, after Catherine and Peter had

In 1744, Princess Sophia Augusta Frederica was brought from Germany to Moscow by horse-drawn sleigh to meet her bridegroom, Grand Duke Peter.

been married for 17 years, Empress Elizabeth died, and Peter was made Emperor of Russia. He was totally unfitted to rule, and the foolish things he did annoyed everybody. Since he had been brought up as a Lutheran, he disliked the Russian Orthodox church, and he took over much of its property. He made his German uncle the commander of the Russian army. He called Catherine a fool in public and threatened to divorce her.

Catherine took these insults patiently, but when a group of Russian army men came to her with a plan to overthrow Peter, she listened willingly. Peter had not been ruling more than six months when the revolution took place. The Russian army officers placed Peter under arrest and demanded that he abdicate the throne. Catherine issued a statement making herself Empress of Russia.

Peter was sent under armed guard to a country house, and a few days later he died. The officers who reported his death to Catherine said that there had been a quarrel at the dinner table and in the fight that followed Peter had been killed. They added that they could not remember exactly what had happened. Catherine announced publicly that

Peter had died of a stroke. Actually, he is believed to have been strangled by a guard.

In September, 1762, Catherine was crowned Empress of Russia. She became known as Catherine the Great because, during the 34 years of her reign, she worked for the enlightenment and improvement of her country.

The 18th century in which Catherine lived was known as the Age of Reason. Because she

A coin made for Catherine's coronation

was an excellent scholar, Catherine corresponded with such men as the French philosopher Voltaire and a group of French scholars who were known as the Encyclopaedists. Influenced by the ideas of these great men, she built hospitals and schools, established the right of women to be educated, introduced vaccination for smallpox in her country, and believed in religious tolerance.

She brought teachers, scientists, and writers from Europe to Russia. She collected works of art and she painted and sculptured herself. She wrote many volumes of prose—her memoirs, a history of Russia, a play, short histories, and an endless series of letters to the intellectuals of Europe. Her energy was enormous.

She would get up at five o'clock in the morning and would work as long as 15 hours a day.

Although her ideas were the liberal ideas of the 18th century, Catherine did not apply them to helping the poorer classes or the peasants in Russia. The Russian peasant was a serf —practically a slave. Catherine needed the support of the nobles among her subjects, and she gave them great power over their serfs. There were many peasant revolts, but Catherine put them down brutally. During the French Revolution, a desire for freedom spread to many parts of the world. There were new peasant uprisings in Russia, and Catherine even exiled her fellow intellectuals who attempted to defend the serfs.

Catherine had a fine army with many able generals and, as commander in chief of this army, she enlarged the kingdom of Russia. She took over parts of Poland and, after two wars with Turkey, she added the Crimea and the lands along the Black Sea to her kingdom. She conquered the uncivilized tribes of Siberia, adding still more territory to Russia.

Catherine lived long enough to see her grandchildren grow up. She died in 1796 of apoplexy and was succeeded by her son Paul.

The coronation of Catherine II as Empress of Russia took place in September, 1762, following the death of her husband, the Emperor Peter, who had ruled for only six months.

Poisonous Plants

Some poisonous plants, like poison ivy, are poisonous only to the touch and cause skin rashes. Others can cause death when taken in large enough doses. However, many poisonous plants are used in medicines because, in small amounts, they can help to cure illnesses, or give comfort. On pages 764 and 765 are some of the best known poisonous plants:

(1) Hemlock looks very much like parsley. It grows in moist, shady places. Water hemlock, or spotted cowbane, as it is sometimes called, is the most poisonous plant that grows in North America. When cattle find nothing else to eat, they sometimes nibble on its leaves and are poisoned.

(2) Nux vomica is the poisonous seed of a bushy plant that grows in Australia, India, Ceylon, and Thailand. Strychnine, a highly poisonous substance, is extracted from the seeds. In very small quantities strychnine is used in medicines for some heart ailments.

(3) Hellebore is a member of the buttercup family and grows wild. It flowers from December to March and is also known as Christmas rose. The underground stem contains a poison called helleborein.

(4) The laurel tree is native to Asia and is cultivated in Europe and North America as an ornamental shrub. The leaves of the tree contain prussic acid, one of the most powerful poisons known. It can cause death in a few moments. The leaves of the laurel tree are sometimes used in medical preparations to calm nervous disturbances.

(5) Nightshade is a climbing plant that grows in moist places. The purple flowers grow in clusters. The fruit, a small purple-red berry, is poisonous. In small doses it is used by doctors to relieve the pain of rheumatism.

(6) Rue, an herb native to Europe, has greenish-yellow flowers. The spotted blue-green leaves have a strong odor and a bitter taste. During the Middle Ages, it was used as a seasoning and in concoctions to ward off evil. In large doses it causes fatal poisoning. In small doses it is used in medicines as a stimulant.

(7) Spurge is a weed that flowers in spring and summer. The stems and leaves are covered with fine hairs and have a milky juice which contains a poisonous substance called euphorbic acid.

(8) Colchicum is also known as meadow saffron. It has violet, funnel-shaped flowers that bloom in late autumn. The seeds contain a poisonous substance called colchicine. In small doses it is used to relieve the symptoms of gout and rheumatism.

(9) Stramonium, also called stinkweed, jimson weed, and thorn apple, is a bad smelling weed that has white, trumpet-shaped flowers. It grows wild in dry, rocky places and empty city lots. It is a member of the nightshade family. Two members of the same family that are not poisonous are tomatoes and potatoes. Stramonium is most poisonous when its seeds appear. In medical preparations it acts as a sedative.

The Greek philosopher Socrates drank a poison made of hemlock to carry out his death sentence.

①   *Hemlock*

Nux vomica   ②

⑥   *Rue*

⑤   *Nightshade*

⑦   *Spurge*

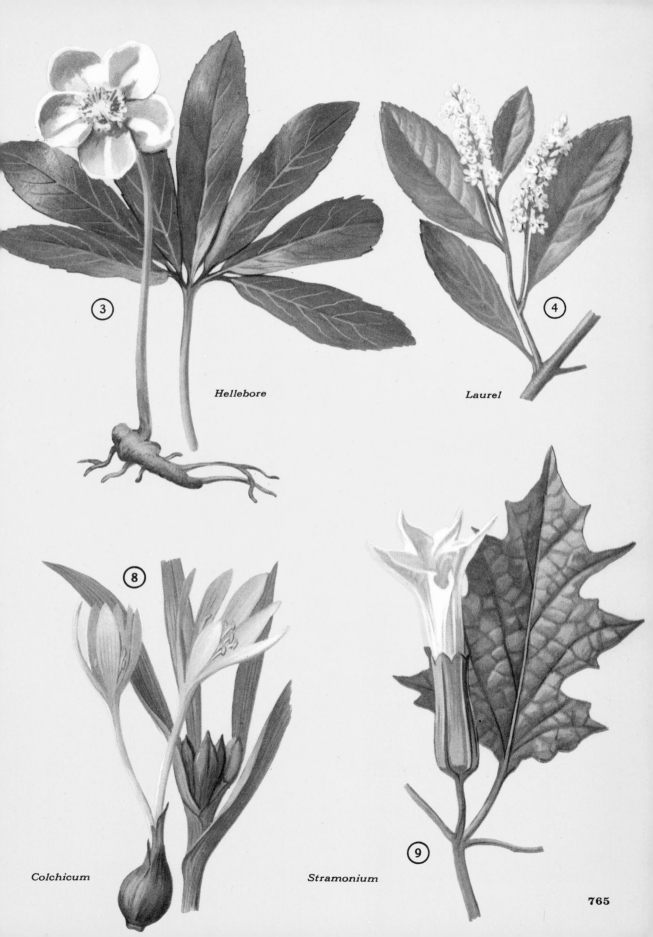

③

Hellebore

④

Laurel

⑧

Colchicum

⑨

Stramonium

765

The Seas

Water covers more than seven-tenths of the surface of the earth. No other planet in our solar system has seas of water such as the earth's. The largest bodies of water are called oceans. Lesser bodies of water are called seas. Enclosed seas are bodies of water which, like the Mediterranean Sea, are almost entirely surrounded by land. The Baltic Sea and the Black Sea are also enclosed seas. Fringing seas such as the China Sea and the North Sea lie next to continents.

Gulfs, like the Gulf of Mexico, are large parts of oceans or seas that extend into land masses.

About three quarters of the earth is covered with water. Only one quarter is land.

A bay is like a gulf, but it is usually smaller. Hudson Bay in northern Canada and the Bay of Biscay off the coast of France are examples.

An inlet is a narrow strip of water running into the land or a narrow channel between islands. A fiord is a long, narrow inlet between high cliffs, such as those along the coast of Norway.

A cove is a small, sheltered inlet or bay. Because coves are sheltered, they usually make good harbors. A lagoon is a shallow body of water partly or completely separated from the sea by a narrow strip of land. A shallow body of water enclosed or nearly enclosed by an atoll is also called a lagoon.

Sounds and straits connect two bodies of water or form channels between the mainland and an island, a group of islands, or a sand bank. Long Island Sound in New York is large, while the Strait of Gibraltar separates two continents by a very narrow channel.

The ocean floor is composed of valleys, plateaus, and mountains. Today, the bottom of the ocean can be mapped just as the land is. Scien-

Continent

Continental shelf

Continental slope

Oce

tists measure the ocean's depth by measuring the time it takes a sound impulse to travel to the bottom and back up to the surface. Scientists have found underwater mountains that rise up from the sea floor in huge ranges. Many islands, such as Hawaii, Bermuda, and the Azores, are the tops of underwater mountains that rise out of the sea.

Enclosed sea

Fringing sea   *Gulf*

The physical features of the ocean bottoms are as different from each other as the continents are. The kind of land under the oceans is divided into three main categories—continental shelves, continental slopes, and the ocean floor. The continental shelves are like plateaus under water. They adjoin all the continents. They are less than 600 feet deep and usually 10 to 200 miles wide. These plateaus slope gently outward from the land masses toward the centers of the oceans.

At the outer edges of the continental shelves the continental slopes begin. They slant abruptly downward to the ocean floor, which averages about 12,500 feet deep. They are not smooth slopes. They are cut by deep gullies and canyons. Not even the deep ocean floor itself is flat. It is a rolling plain, interrupted by underwater mountains.

The deepest parts of the oceans are not in the ocean floor in the center of the ocean basins. They are found close to the continental land masses. These deeps are called trenches, and are formed from breaks which make great chasms in the continental shelf. Some trenches are several miles down from the surface of the sea. Two of the deepest trenches are in the Pacific Ocean. They are more than 35,500 feet deep!

Until recently there was little knowledge about the depths of the ocean since there was no way man could go down that far under water. Today, explorations are being conducted by means of a bathyscaph—a self-propelled sort of diving bell—which has carried men seven miles down under the sea safely. Now, underwater trenches, shelves, and mountains

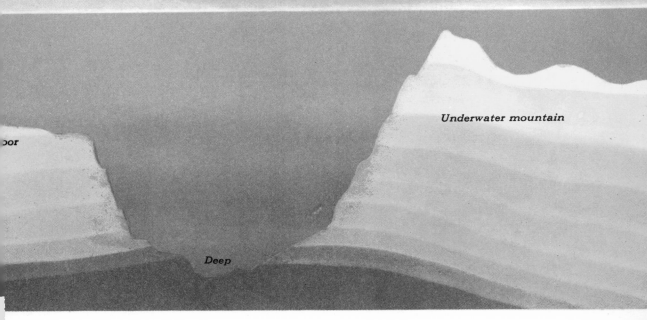

Underwater mountain

Deep

are being explored in many places in the world.

In the seas there are many land masses other than continents and large islands. Reefs are outcroppings of rock near the coast of a mainland. Reefs can be large or small. Unless they are marked, they are often dangerous to shipping, particularly when high tides cover them with water. Shoals are similar to reefs. They may be rock or a sand bar. All of them are high places under the sea that nearly reach the surface of the water. They are covered at high tide, but sometimes show at low tide.

Atolls are reefs made of coral, usually circular or horseshoe-shaped, and surrounding a lagoon. Many islands in the South Pacific are of the atoll type. An archipelago may be a group of islands or a series of atolls.

The tides are controlled by the pull of the sun and the moon on the sea. This causes the level of the water to rise and fall against the land masses all over the world. The tide changes in most places twice a day. High tide is called the flood tide and low tide is the ebb tide. In some places the water rises only a few feet, but in the Bay of Fundy, off the coast of Canada, the tide rises as high as 70 feet.

The swell of the sea is a series of parallel waves in the open sea. Surf is the wave that breaks upon the shore. A surge or billow is a very high wave—a great rolling swell of water. A breaker is a wave that breaks into foam over a rock or sand bar.

The lands around the seas have special names, too. The coast, or seaboard, is the land that edges the sea. Coasts may be cliffs of high, steep rock rising directly from the sea, or low, flat, sandy beaches. The shape of a seacoast gives it the name promontory, peninsula, cape, or isthmus. A promontory is a high peak of land that juts out over the sea. A peninsula is larger than a promontory, and it is nearly surrounded by water. A cape is larger than a promontory, but not as big as a peninsula. A cape is sometimes called a point if it is rocky and pointed, or a tongue if it is low and sandy. An isthmus is a narrow strip of land with water on two sides that unites two larger pieces of land, like the Isthmus of Panama that joins North and South America.

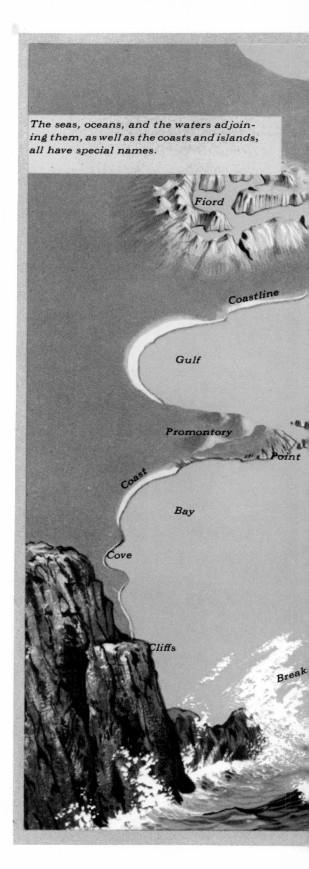

The seas, oceans, and the waters adjoining them, as well as the coasts and islands, all have special names.

Fiord

Coastline

Gulf

Promontory

Point

Coast

Bay

Cove

Cliffs

Break

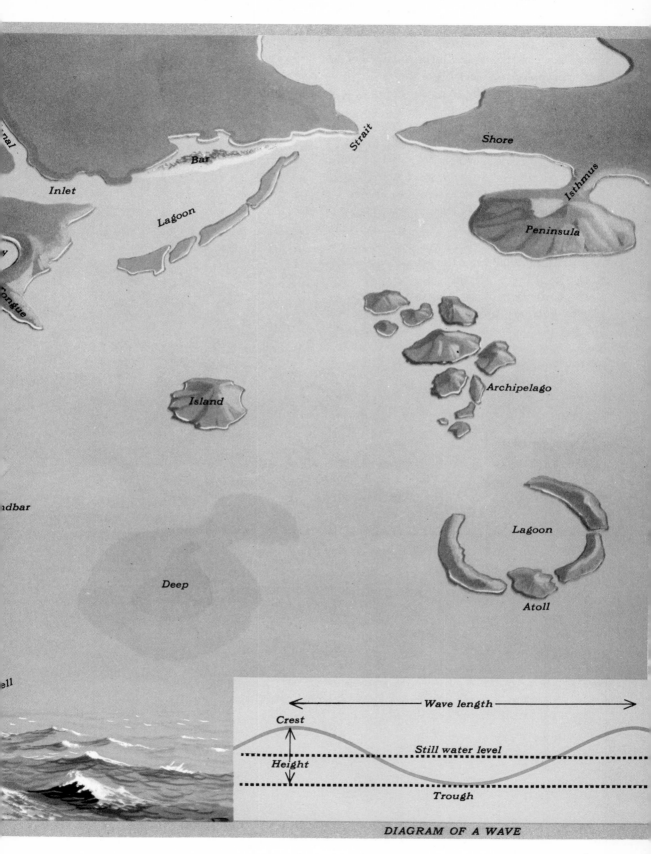

Strait

Shore

Bar

Isthmus

Inlet

Peninsula

Lagoon

nal

Tongue

Archipelago

Island

ndbar

Lagoon

Deep

Atoll

ell

Wave length

Crest

Still water level

Height

Trough

DIAGRAM OF A WAVE

The Negro Peoples of Africa

Every day the newspapers carry stories about the new African nations which are gaining their independence and joining the United Nations. The articles tell how the new nations are struggling to get themselves organized, to elect leaders, and to unite and educate their peoples for a better future life.

To understand Africa, it is helpful to understand something about its many different types of people.

The population of the world is divided into three main groups—Caucasoid, Mongoloid, and Negroid. Of these groups, the Negro group is much the smallest. About 150,000,000 of the world's Negroes live in Africa. Negroes also live in Asia and, of course, the Americas.

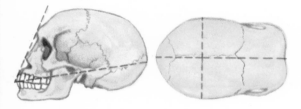

The Negroid skull is characteristically long and has a more sloping forehead than the Caucasoid.

Although the various African peoples are vastly different from one another, there is still a characteristic Negro type, just as there is a characteristic yellow or white type. In general, pure-blooded Negroes have dark, shiny skin, heavy lips, broad noses, sloping foreheads, and woolly hair. Their skulls are shaped differently from the skulls of white or yellow peoples. Of all the peoples in Africa, the Sudanese who live on the plains of the Sudan, are the purest example of the Negroid type, unmixed with any other race.

The Watusi tribe, another strongly Negroid type, live in the Congo. They are rarely less than six feet six inches tall, and are an extremely handsome people. They have slim, oval faces, thin lips, and slender, well-proportioned bodies. They are also one of the most highly civilized of the Central African peoples. They originally came from the valley of the Nile, and they moved into the Congo in search of slaves to till their fields and take care of their cattle.

Today, the Watusi are still good farmers, and they still have servants to do much of their hard work. They do not eat meat, but live on milk, bananas, beans, and potatoes. They are skillful high jumpers.

Many of the peoples of Africa are a mixture of races. For example, the people of Ethiopia and Somaliland are a mixture of Negro and white. They are dark-skinned, but have few other Negro characteristics. Their features are fine and their foreheads do not slope. Their customs and beliefs are more European than African. And unlike most Africans, they are practitioners of the Christian religions.

The most numerous African race is the Bantus. The name Bantu comes from the language

The tall Watusi tribesmen of Central Africa are graceful dancers and high-jumpers.

which all these Negroes originally spoke. The Bantus are divided into tribes such as the Zulus and Swahilis. These Negroes look a lot like the Sudanese, but many have thinner lips and slenderer noses. By tradition, Bantus are farmers and cattle raisers. But now many of them work in the diamond mines and in other businesses owned by white men. Contact with their employers has modernized the lives of many Bantus, and it is now an ordinary sight to see a Bantu man in western clothes pedaling to work on a bicycle.

African Negro jewelry, weapons, woven objects and sculpture are often beautifully designed.

What the Pygmies lack in size they make up for in speed and hunting skill.

771

THE NEGRO PEOPLES OF AFRICA

South of the Bantus live the Bushmen and the Hottentots. Neither of these groups is pure Negro because their ancestors belonged to both the black and yellow races. Bushmen and Hottentots have yellowish-brown skin and they are short, well built, and strong. Many Bushmen and Hottentots live on the Kalahari Desert, where life is very hard. The Hottentots are cattle raisers who live together in tribes. They do not move very often. They stay in one place and care for their cattle and farms so that they will have food and milk during the dry seasons.

The Bushmen, a very primitive people, are nomadic hunters who wander from place to place in search of food and water. They do not farm, but eat whatever they can find—wild grass, roots, and fruit. They get most of their

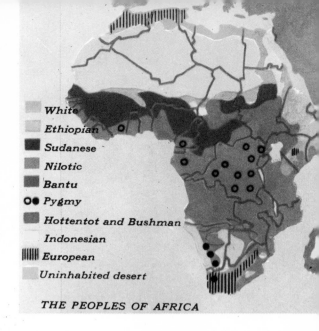

White
Ethiopian
Sudanese
Nilotic
Bantu
Pygmy
Hottentot and Bushman
Indonesian
European
Uninhabited desert

THE PEOPLES OF AFRICA

water from the underground roots of desert plants, or by sticking thin hollow canes into the ground and sucking up the water from underground streams. They kill wild animals with poisoned arrows and then divide the meat among the members of the band. Each band wanders in its own hunting ground. Bushmen wear very little clothing and they have no houses. They sleep in hollows they dig in the ground. A group of these hollows is the only kind of village the people have.

Deep in the jungles of the Congo live the Pygmies. They are supposed to have lived in Africa longer than any other Negroes, but they are so shy that white men seldom see them. Pygmies are usually not more than four and a half feet tall. They have brown skin and their faces and bodies are very hairy. Besides being small, they are also very quick. They run away from enemies and they also chase the animals they hunt. Pygmies are also clever at trapping and they catch much of their food this way. They have no villages, but move constantly in search of game.

As Africa becomes more civilized, ancient practices such as cannibalism are dying out. The witch doctor with his magic is less feared and respected than he used to be. The concern of Africans is more with government and education than with black magic. In fact, the Dark Continent is becoming less a mysterious land of savages and more a rich land of educated men.

Somalis have delicate, almost feminine features.

African painted pottery

Glass

The art of making glass is very old. Small objects made of rough glass have been found in ancient Egyptian tombs built in 4000 B.C. During the first century A.D., the Romans made cups, bottles, and vases of glass. They even began to make plate glass for windows.

With the fall of the Roman Empire, the art of glassmaking moved east to Constantinople. Italian traders from Venice brought the secrets of glassmaking back to Italy. The Venetian glassmakers invented new ways of working with glass and were so proud of their fine glassware that they kept their methods secret for many years. As time passed, glassmakers in other Italian cities learned the secrets of Venetian glass. They taught the methods to glassmakers in England, France, and other countries in Europe.

During the 17th century, many countries were producing glass very similar to the original Venetian glass. And soon they began to develop glass that was heavier and more highly decorated. By the 18th century glassmaking became an established industry in the United States, some of the best being produced in Pennsylvania. And in the 19th century in the village of Sandwich, on Cape Cod, artists were turning out glassware in beautiful shapes and colors. Sandwich glass is valuable today and is displayed in museums.

During the 19th century, glassmaking increased as an industry. New machines made mass production of glass possible. Discoveries in chemistry led to a wider range of uses for glass because its chemical composition could be controlled. By varying the ingredients, glassmakers could make glass suitable for many different uses. Scientists found ways to make glass almost unbreakable. They discovered how to make glass that could hold chemicals without being affected by them.

Glass is made of a mixture of raw materials which have been heated to almost 1,300 degrees Fahrenheit. These raw materials fuse and, when they are cooled, harden into glass.

The Romans made vases and pitchers of glass.

The secrets of beautiful Venetian glass were jealously kept for many years.

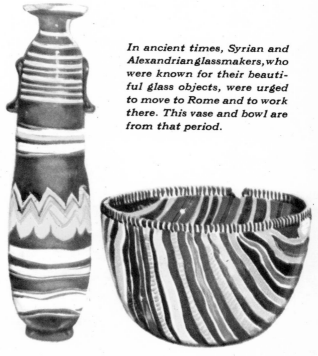

In ancient times, Syrian and Alexandrian glassmakers, who were known for their beautiful glass objects, were urged to move to Rome and to work there. This vase and bowl are from that period.

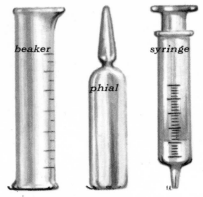

Glass containers used for scientific purposes must be made in a way that makes them acid resistant.

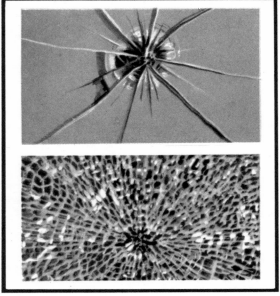

Tempered glass may splinter and crack, but it will not break into jagged, dangerous pieces.

The main ingredients of glass are silica, alkali, and lime. There is more silica than anything else. Silica is sand—either rock crystal or quartz. It is this melted sand that becomes glass. An alkali is added to make the silica melt at a lower temperature. The alkalis usually used are sodas, sodium sulphate, and potash. Since alkalis make the sand melt easily, glass made only of silica and alkali would melt in boiling water. Lime is added to the mixture to balance the effect of the alkali so the finished glass will not melt so easily.

In addition to silica, alkali, and lime, other substances are added to the heated mixture in much smaller amounts. Minerals are added to make the glass clearer or brighter or to add color, strength, or other properties. Crystal is a clear and bright kind of glass. It is also fine and thin and therefore breaks easily. A crystal champagne glass is different from an ordinary drinking glass. And yet they are both made of silica, alkali, and lime. The difference is that lead oxide has been added to crystal.

Boric oxide is added to some glass to make it heat resistant. Such cooking utensils as coffee pots, baking dishes, and many laboratory implements are made from glass that has been treated in this way. In making chemists' test tubes, flasks, and beakers, which must not be affected by acids, more alkali than usual is added to the silica and lime mixture.

When the molten raw materials have fused into glass, the glass is handled according to

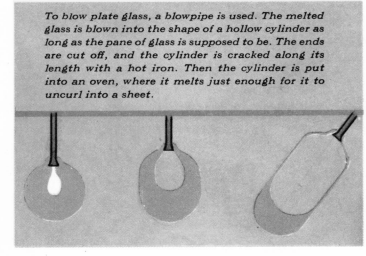

To blow plate glass, a blowpipe is used. The melted glass is blown into the shape of a hollow cylinder as long as the pane of glass is supposed to be. The ends are cut off, and the cylinder is cracked along its length with a hot iron. Then the cylinder is put into an oven, where it melts just enough for it to uncurl into a sheet.

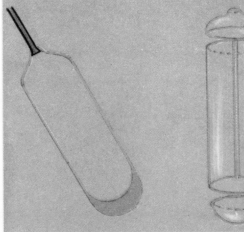

is blown into from the other end, producing a pear shaped bubble. By swinging, twisting, or rolling the pipe, the bubble can be shaped. In large glassmaking factories, the bubble is usually blown right into a mold of the desired shape. When the glass has hardened, it is broken off the pipe and its edges are smoothed.

The easiest and fastest way to make sheet glass is to pour it in a flat sheet and buff it.

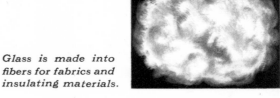

Glass is made into fibers for fabrics and insulating materials.

glass   crystal

Crystal is brighter and clearer than ordinary glass.

what is to be made. Hollow objects, such as bottles and vases, are usually blown. Blowing is the oldest way of handling glass. It may be done by hand or by machine. A blowpipe is dipped in the molten glass. It picks up enough glass for the object that is to be made. The pipe

Today whole buildings are walled with glass brick.

Early glass-blowing was usually done by hand.

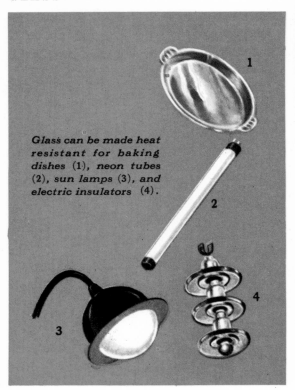

Glass can be made heat resistant for baking dishes (1), neon tubes (2), sun lamps (3), and electric insulators (4).

Plate glass, which is used for windowpanes, can also be blown. But nowadays plate glass is usually poured. Melted glass is poured onto a metal-edged table and spread evenly. It is smoothed out by huge rollers. It is ground and polished when it must be made especially smooth and clear. For grinding, sand is put between the rollers and the glass. For polishing, felt covers are put on the rollers. The glass is cooled slowly and then cut into panes.

Some sheet glass is not cooled slowly. Tempered glass is cooled quickly, so that the outer layers of the sheet harden more quickly than the inside. This process of tempering produces sheet glass that is stronger than ordinary sheet glass. Tempered glass is not unbreakable, but when it is hit hard, it cracks or splinters instead of breaking into large jagged pieces. For this reason, tempered glass is called safety glass, and is used for automobile windows.

At one time glass was made only by hand. It was expensive and only the wealthy could afford to buy it. Today glass is available to everyone and is used in everything from cloth made from glass fibers to buildings made of glass bricks.

Galen

One day many years ago a famous Persian philosopher visited a doctor in Rome. The Persian complained that he had lost all feeling in two of his fingers. None of the treatments he had tried seemed to help, the philosopher explained. The doctor examined him and asked, "Have you ever hurt your back?" The philosopher remembered that years before a stone had fallen and hurt the middle of his back. "But what does that have to do with my fingers?" he asked.

The doctor explained that the stone had caused an inflammation in the man's spine. That is where the nerve which controls the fingers begins. The old accident was responsible for this present lack of feeling.

This happened in the year A.D. 171. The doctor was Galen, and he made the same diagnosis almost 1,800 years ago that a doctor would make today.

Galen was born in Pergamum, on the shores of the Mediterranean, early in the second century. He studied philosophy and medicine, which were considered to be much alike at that time. He traveled to Corinth and Alexandria to study further. When he returned to Pergamum, at the age of 28, he was already a well-known doctor.

During the next few years he treated many gladiators when they were wounded. This was a wonderful opportunity for a doctor in those days, because autopsies—the dissection of the dead—was forbidden, and doctors had few opportunities to study the human body. Most of Galen's studies and observations up to that time had been made while working with animals.

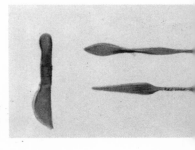

Roman surgical instruments used in Galen's time.

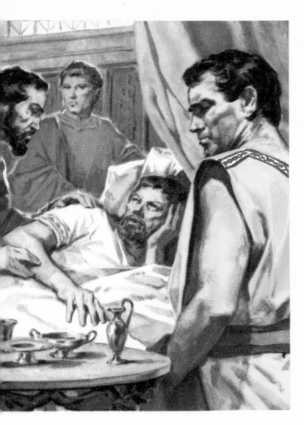

Because of intensive study in the way the body works, Galen was able to diagnose successfully the illnesses of Marcus Aurelius, the Emperor.

However, at the gladiator school, treating wounded men, he was able to learn a great deal about human muscles, nerves, and bones.

As a result of his studies of human anatomy, Galen was the first man in the history of medicine to make a distinction between the nerves that enable us to feel things and the nerves that enable us to move our bodies. Galen also realized that there was a continuous circulatory system in the body that carried blood and other liquids to and from all its parts. Be-

cause most of his experiments were performed on the bodies of animals, however, Galen did make some mistakes. But hundreds of years passed before others knew enough to realize what the mistakes were.

Galen eventually left Pergamum and went to the great city of Rome, where his fame spread. His lectures in public theaters were attended by important people. And even the Emperor himself, Marcus Aurelius, became one of his patients.

Galen's writings were very popular even in his own day and were translated into Greek and Arabic. One of the subjects he wrote about was the danger of magic cures and self-styled doctors. In those days no license was required to practice medicine, and Galen charged that "even the shoemakers and ironmongers . . . are passing for doctors." He warned people of the danger of relying on untrained physicians.

Hippocrates, the Greek scientist who is called the founder of medicine, believed that there are four humors in our bodies. If one of these humors became stronger than the others, Hippocrates believed, it would affect a man's temperament and finally make him ill. Galen didn't believe this. He believed that illnesses had specific physical causes. And he based his opinions on what he had been able to observe directly. Because of his careful research and his emphasis on facts, Galen has been called the first modern doctor. His name in Latin was Galenus, and the people of his own time rearranged the letters to spell *Angelus,* because he was thought of as the angel of medicine.

In the last years of his life Galen summed up his life's work in his most important book, *The Art of Medicine.* This book was a standard textbook for students until 1660.

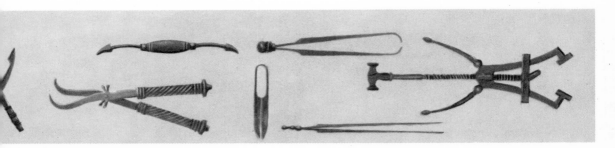

The three dancers shown here are a Greek dancer accompanying himself on a stringed instrument, an African doing a war dance before a battle, and a Siamese witch doctor dancing to drive evil spirits out of the body of his patient.

Dance through the Ages

Dancing has always been one of the most natural ways of expressing feelings. A dancer can communicate with people who do not even speak his language. It is the first of the arts that was developed by primitive men. Cave drawings in Spain made 10,000 years ago show men dancing around animals, in what was probably a hunting dance.

Primitive man celebrated births, marriages, and battle victories by dancing. They would also dance religious rituals to try to influence their gods. They thought they could overcome wars, sickness, bad crops, and death by dancing to frighten away evil spirits. In war dances, the men waved their weapons and pretended to attack the enemy. They hoped this acting would make them braver and bring them victory when the battle took place.

The dancing of primitive men was usually wild and exuberant. The whole body was used at once, as drums beat the rhythm. As men became more civilized, their dances became more formal. The Greeks considered dancing an art form, and men were trained carefully. Dancing was combined with music and singing, and it is from these early performances that the famous Greek dramatic tragedies for festivals developed.

A number of different dances were developed by the Greeks for special occasions. The *pyrrhic* was a war dance performed with a sword and a spear. It was thought that the best

Prehistoric paintings on rocks in the Sahara Desert show a ritual dance that was done thousands of years ago.

An African witch doctor dances to save a sick person from evil spirits.

Greek warriors performing a pyrrhic *dance which was named for Pyrrhus, son of Achilles.*

Greeks danced the slow, tragic emmeleia *during the tragic plays performed at festivals.*

dancer would also be the best fighter. The *emmeleia* was danced slowly and was performed in tragic scenes. The *sikinnis* originated as a dance to please the gods of agriculture. It was later performed during Satyric dramas, in which the dancers were dressed like satyrs, with goat skins covering their legs. Satyrs were woodland gods which were represented as half man and half goat. The *kordax* was danced by two people to the accompaniment of castanets.

The Romans did not dance themselves. They imported dancers into Rome from other countries they had conquered. The Romans especially enjoyed spectacles with many per-

cepted as an art once again. Among the dances that were adopted at the royal courts of Europe was the gavotte, a graceful dance which was popular until the 19th century. The minuet began as a folk dance. In a more elegant and formal version, it became popular at European courts in the 17th century. The rhythm of the minuet was so pleasing that Chopin, Beethoven, and Mozart adopted the style in some of their music.

In the 19th century the waltz became popular throughout Europe. It was simple to learn, so people did not need lessons to enjoy it. Famous composers like Strauss wrote waltzes,

The sikinnis *was danced to please the gods of agriculture.*

A couple danced the kordax, *the most popular folk dance of early Greece. The woman beat time with castanets.*

formers and a great deal of action. One of the arts they imported was the pantomime. In this, the performers acted silently telling a story in gestures and dancing. These pantomimes were the basis of ballet, which was developed hundreds of years later.

During the Middle Ages, dance forms that had been developed earlier all but disappeared. They were connected with earlier religions, and the Christian church disapproved of them. But although there was very little theatre dancing, folk dancing became a popular social event. Folk dances are gay and lively, and many people can take part in them. In time, these dances were adopted by the nobility, who transformed them into more formal and stately dances. Dancing teachers appeared for the first time at the end of the Middle Ages, so that rich merchants could learn the dances of the nobility.

In the Renaissance liveliness was again introduced into dancing, and the dance was ac-

and these tunes are still hummed and played today. The polka is a Bohemian dance that originated in the 19th century. From Poland there came two popular dances, the mazurka and the polonnaise.

Today, the influence of jazz from the United States has had a great effect on social dancing throughout most of the world. South American

Roman pantomimists often wore masks.

The gavotte was popular in the 18th century.

The waltz was a dance that everyone could do and it swept Europe in the 19th century.

Minuets became so popular that many great composers wrote music for them.

music and dancing has been adopted in Western Europe and North America, and tangos and rhumbas are popular in most countries.

Ballet originated at the court balls held in Italy during the Renaissance. These royal entertainments included elaborate pantomimes and dances performed by the members of the court. Louis XIV of France became very interested in ballet as it was then danced. He studied with the best teachers, and became the best dancer at his court. He encouraged others to develop their skills, and ballet became a serious art in the 17th century. Louis established the Academy of Dance in 1661 as a school for training dancers.

At this time, court performers gradually were replaced by carefully trained professional dancers. The five positions of the feet, which are still the basis of every movement in ballet dancing, were originated in 1680. Around 1700, women first appeared in these professional pro-

The polka was originally a folk dance.

The mazurka originated in Poland.

ductions. Silent ballets were first danced in the early 18th century. Up to that time ballet had been interrupted with intervals of dialogue.

Choreographers played an important part in making up new stories and scenes. They were expected to create new ballets for special occasions and for holidays at court. In the 19th century, ballet had already become a popular art and it could be seen in theatres, instead of being confined to the courts. Women first began to dance on their toes at this time. Long romantic ballets with complicated plots and dozens of characters were created.

Ballet styles change as the years go by. In the 19th century, classical ballet was popular.

In the early part of the 20th century, Isadora Duncan started what has been called Modern Dance. She said that dancers should try to express their feelings, not just follow old-fashioned steps and stories. The three-hour plots of the 19th century gave way to many ballets which express a particular mood, without a specific story. New choreographers have created ballets that are more in keeping with our times, and are danced to modern music. Dancers also use their bodies in movements that have not been tried before, although all their dance steps still have their origin in the older and more formal movements of ballet.

In the United States three of the best-known choreographers are Martha Graham, George Balanchine, and Jerome Robbins. Each specializes in one field. Miss Graham is known for her pioneering in the more angular modern dance field. Balanchine is a leading choreographer in ballet, and Robbins is best known for his jazz style in Broadway shows.

Lead

Lead is one of the most useful metals known to man. It was known to the Egyptians and the ancient Babylonians, who used it to make bracelets and necklaces. The Romans used lead to make water pipes for their aqueducts, baths, and private houses. Lead is so durable that today, in the English city of Bath, parts of lead pipes made by the Romans are still being used. The pipes were made almost 2,000 years ago. In North America, lead was one of

Lead sulfide—called galena—is the commonest form of lead.

the first metals mined by the colonists. They needed it to make bullets for hunting.

Lead is rarely found free or pure in nature. It is usually mixed with other elements such as sulfur, silver, copper, and zinc. Lead is found in many places in the world. The main deposits are in Missouri, Idaho, Colorado, and in Australia, Mexico, Canada, the U.S.S.R., and Peru. More than 2,000,000 tons of lead are mined in the world each year.

Lead is a heavy metal. It is 11 times as heavy as water. It is silver in color when freshly cut with a knife, but it will turn darker in moist air because of a film of lead oxide that forms on its surface. The lead oxide appears when the lead joins with the oxygen in the air. But lead does not rust, as iron does, so lead is useful in making water pipes.

Lead is a soft metal and it can be hammered into various shapes. It melts easily and can be poured into molds, but it cannot be drawn into thin wires. Lead is not strong and it breaks easily when it is thinned out.

Lead is very useful today because it absorbs

atomic radiation. Used in thick, heavy sheets, lead will protect a man from radioactive substances. At the same time, lead can be dangerous because it is highly poisonous. People who stay in rooms where there are lead vapors or lead powders can get lead poisoning by inhaling it. Workers who make lead batteries, printers who handle lead type, and painters who use lead paint must be careful to avoid inhaling the lead fumes. Objects that babies might chew are no longer painted with lead paint because of the danger of poisoning.

USES OF LEAD COMPOUNDS

(1) *Printing type is made with a mixture of lead, antimony, and tin.* (2) *Bearings can be made of lead alloy.* (3) *The pellets in a shotgun are made from a lead-arsenic alloy.* (4) *A tube of white lead* (5) *A bucket of red lead* (6) *Many storage batteries have lead-antimony plates.*

USES OF PURE LEAD

(1) *Lead chamber towers are used in the industrial production of sulfuric acid.* (2) *Electric cables are insulated with lead.* (3) *Lead is used for sealing such things as freight car doors and packages.* (4) *Lead crucibles are used in chemical laboratories.*

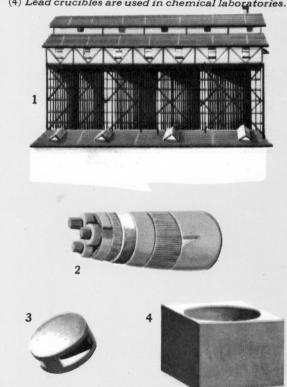

The lead in pencils is actually not lead at all but graphite, which is a compound of carbon.

According to legend, the ancient Spartans in Greece made money out of lead. They found the weight of many coins discouraged people from hoarding them. In the Middle Ages, lead was often used to cover roofs. Later on, it was used to make the type used in printing books. Since lead combines with other substances, it is a part of a great many chemicals used in industry today. Red lead and white lead are the names given to the lead compounds that are used in making paints, car storage batteries, and glass. Lead compounds are added to gasoline so that the fuel will burn more slowly. If there were no lead in the gasoline, car engines would develop more knocks than they do.

Trawlers are used in commercial deep sea fishing. They are able to stay out at sea for over a month.

Fishing

Fish is one of man's most important foods, and fishing provides a livelihood for thousands of people all over the world. Many people fish for fun, but commercial fishing is a widespread and profitable business. Every year millions of tons of fish are caught in the lakes, rivers, and oceans of the world. Some of this fish is sold fresh. Even more is frozen, canned, or smoked so that it can be stored for later use. Some fresh-water fish are caught commercially, but fishing at sea is the more important part of the industry.

Fishing with a rod and reel is more often done for pleasure than as a way of making a living.

The circled areas are major fishing zones in which trawlers from many nations operate.

There are three main kinds of sea fishing, depending upon the distance of the fishing grounds from the mainland. Coastal fishing is done within 50 miles of the coasts. Fishing on the continental shelf is done 50 to 300 miles offshore. Deep sea fishing takes place hundreds or thousands of miles from land.

Special boats called trawlers are used in commercial deep sea fishing. They can stay far out at sea for over a month and can hold thousands of pounds of fish. The fish are caught in

huge trawl nets towed under water by the boats. Trawlers are usually equipped with refrigerated holds for preserving the catch and with modern electronic devices to detect the presence of schools of fish. Some of the larger boats even carry helicopters, which also help find fish. Trawlers of many nations are found in the North Sea, the Newfoundland Banks of the Atlantic, and in the Arctic Ocean.

Coastal and offshore fishing boats are usually smaller than deep sea fishing boats, and they do not remain on the fishing grounds as long. Offshore boats make trips of one and two weeks. Coastal boats—such as small draggers, shrimpers, and lobster boats—often return to port each evening.

Commercial trawlers are able to remain at sea for long periods of time. Some freeze their catch and some transfer the fish to other boats which carry them ashore to the canneries.

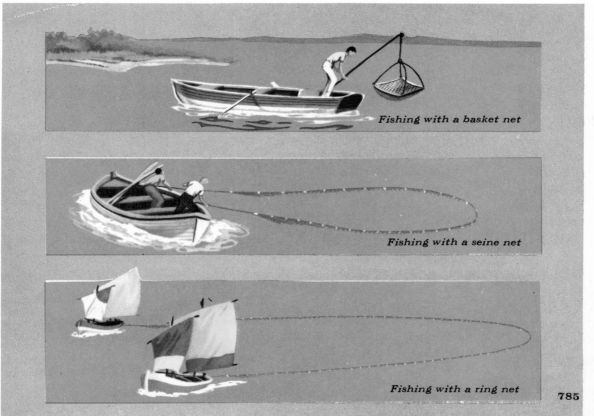

Fishing with a basket net

Fishing with a seine net

Fishing with a ring net

The hook and line, spear, and trap were used for fishing by primitive man. Today modern forms of them are still used. Most fishing with hook and line today is done for sport and not for profit. But some fish, such as cod and halibut, are commercially caught on hook and line. Large fish, such as swordfish and giant tuna, are often harpooned. But today most commercial fishing is done with nets.

Basket nets, seine nets, or ring nets are dropped into the water from boats and pulled aboard when they are filled with fish. Some fish can be found in shallow water. These are caught by groups of men who wade or row out into the ocean or river with a big net. The men drag the loaded net directly to shore.

Off the coast of Florida and in other southern waters, deep sea fishing is a popular sport. Swordfish, marlin, tarpon, and other big fish are caught with a heavy rod and line from the deck of a large motor boat. There is often a long struggle to land these strong fish.

In the sport of skin diving, men breathing through portable air tanks find and follow small fish under the water and kill them with special harpoons. Along some of the European, African, and Asian coasts, large fish are killed with harpoons. The Eskimos of Greenland also catch seals in this way.

Off the shores of Malaya and Indochina, huge fish traps are made of rows of tree trunks. These are sunk into the sea bed and joined together with bamboo fencing. The fish swim into a series of chambers, where they are trapped. In many African rivers, such as the Niger and the Congo, the people make a fence of branches, reeds, and willows, and place it where the current is strongest. The fish, carried along by the current, are caught on the fence. The fishermen dive into the swirling waters to collect them by hand.

Some large fish are caught with harpoons.

A fish trap in a Malayan river

A fish fence in an African river

Animals of the World

Animals are found all over the world, from the ice-covered polar regions to the rain forests of the equatorial regions. An animal adjusts in size, shape, coloring, diet, intelligence, or structure to a particular environment. This is called adaptation. In order to survive, animals adapt themselves to the conditions of the area in which they live.

Two things affecting the distribution of animals in the world are natural barriers and temperatures. Oceans acted as a natural barrier to prevent animals from reaching New Zealand, until they were brought there by man. Animals have also moved from one area to another as rivers have changed course and forests have been destroyed.

The earth's climate zones are determined by the average temperature and the amount of rain that falls. The five main climate zones of the earth are the humid tropical, the dry tropical, the warm temperate, the cold temperate, and the polar.

The humid tropical zone is very hot and wet, and the land is covered with jungles and rain forests. The zone lies in a belt on both sides of the equator and includes a large part of South America, Central Africa, some of India, and most of the islands of Southeast Asia. Animals in this zone include monkeys, elephants, tigers, and crocodiles.

The dry tropical zone is also very hot. The temperature climbs to over 100 degrees Fahrenheit during the day. There is so little rain that most of the land is desert.

In adapting to life under such conditions, desert animals are able to go for long periods of time without water. As protection against the hot sun, they have fewer skin glands, and their bodies manufacture water by breaking down carbohydrates. Many animals hide in burrows until the sun goes down and the sand has cooled. Lizards, such as the chameleon and the Gila monster, hide under rocks during the day. Because there are few natural hiding places, the color of many desert animals is almost the same as that of the soil.

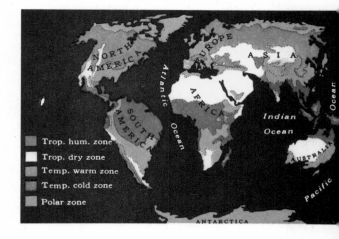

Trop. hum. zone
Trop. dry zone
Temp. warm zone
Temp. cold zone
Polar zone

The warm temperate zone lies between the hot and cold, and wet and dry climate. Many animals natural to the warm temperate zone, such as the buffalo in North America, have been driven out by the advance of civilization. Other animals, such as house rats and mice, have followed man almost everywhere he has settled. Some animals in the temperate zone, such as the horse and the dog, have been tamed. Other animals in this zone include deer, wolves, bears, rabbits, ducks, geese, and wildcats.

The cold temperate zone has long winters with ice and snow much of the year. Animals in this zone have a nearly constant body temperature and thick fur that enable them to withstand the extreme cold. Some animals hibernate, so they need thick layers of fat. In hibernation, their metabolism slows down and their body temperature drops almost to that of the surrounding climate. Grizzly bears, polar bears, reindeer, and snowshoe rabbits are found in this area.

The extreme northern and southern parts of the earth are polar zones. They are covered with ice throughout the year and, as a result, have very few plants. Plant-eating polar animals have hoofs, teeth, or claws adapted to removing the ice that covers the sparse vegetation. Many flesh-eating polar animals, such as seals, penguins, and sea lions, get their food from the sea, and are excellent fishermen.

The pictures of these animals are not drawn to scale

During the course of time in every climate of the world the animals have developed characteristics to enable them to withstand the rigors of that particular climate. The polar bear, for example, has his extremely thick coat to protect him from the arctic cold. And the camel is able to store water under his skin and in his muscles as a reserve against water shortages in the desert.

Snow Finch
Reindeer
Wolf
Brown Bear
Marmot
Wolf
Red Deer
Beaver
Otter
Wolf
Eagle
Crane
Yak
Cormorant
Moufflon Sheep
Pig
Camel
Japanese Salamander
Crocodile
Elephant
Tiger
Eagle
Ostrich
Indian Elephant
Seagull
Tiger
Cobra
Indian Rhinoceros
Hammerhead Shark
Giraffe
Orangutan
Hippopotamus
Shark
Green Turtle
Rhinoceros
Ray
Dolphin
Kudu
Cayman
Frilled Lizard
Sea Lion
Kangaroo
Sperm Whale
Seal

789

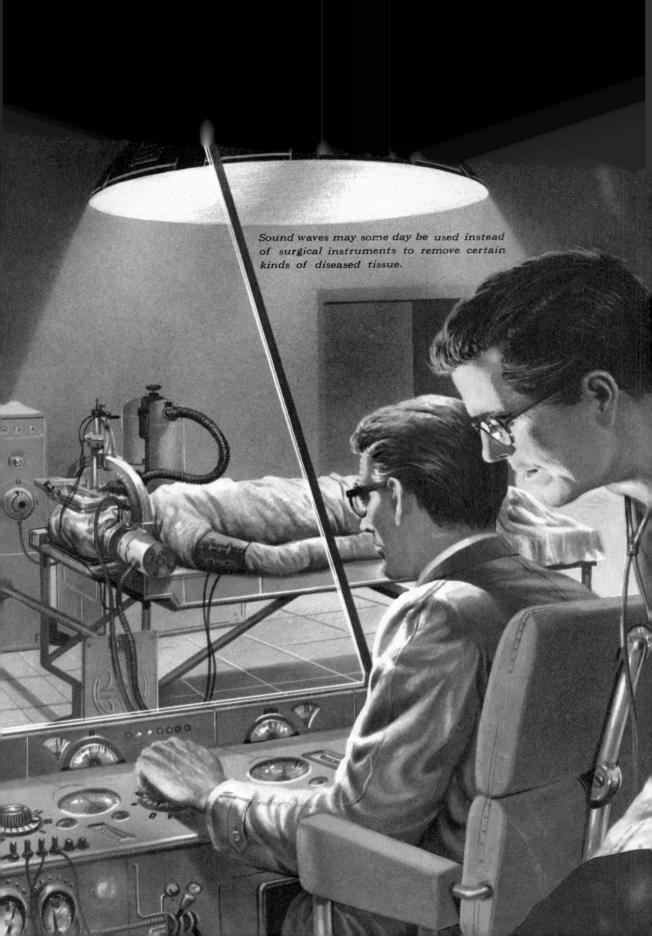

Sound waves may some day be used instead of surgical instruments to remove certain kinds of diseased tissue.

Surgery

Surgery is the branch of medicine that repairs the human body by operating on it.

The story of surgery goes back nearly 10,000 years. Skeletons have been found that show brain surgery was performed in ancient times. Surgery was also used to repair battle injuries such as arrowhead wounds and broken bones. An Egyptian painting dating back to 2500 B.C. actually shows a surgical operation in progress. By the second century A.D., surgeons in India had developed methods for performing plastic surgery by grafting skin from one part of the body to another.

Modern surgery, however, became possible only after scientific studies of the body had been made. The Greek physician Hippocrates, in the fifth century B.C., is believed to have been the first to study human anatomy. But it was not until the 16th century that the first accurate anatomical studies were made.

In 1543 the Italian surgeon and anatomist Vesalius published the first book describing and illustrating human anatomy. Another important contribution to surgery was the Englishman William Harvey's description of the circulation of the blood in the human body. Modern surgery is based on man's increasing knowledge of the body's structure.

The 18th-century English surgeons John and William Hunter are considered to be the first scientific surgeons. Their studies in anatomy, pathology, and physiology brought about the development of many new techniques and instruments for surgical use. In the United States surgery has taken giant steps forward. Among the most famous American surgeons are William Beaumont, William Halsted, and Harvey Cushing.

Until the middle of the 19th century, a surgical operation was a dreaded and painful experience for the patient. Up to this time the physicians had only a few ways to reduce pain. They depended mostly upon alcohol and opium compounds. These drugs relieved pain only slightly and for a short while.

The development of drugs called general anesthetics in the United States in the 1840's made it possible for the surgeon to work more slowly and for the patient to undergo his operation painlessly. Nitrous oxide—laughing gas—chloroform, and ether were the three most commonly used general anesthetics. They are still used today. These drugs, and others that have been developed more recently, are inhaled through a mask placed over the face. Other kinds of general anesthetics are given to the patient by injection.

There are local anesthetics too. These stop pain only near the place of injection. Procaine, which is used in dentistry, is a local anes-

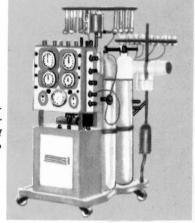

A special machine is used for giving general anesthesia to the patient.

thetic. Local anesthetics which are injected into the spinal column have been developed for abdominal operations.

The development of anesthesia made it possible for operations to be painless, but a great danger remained—infection. The most famous name in the war against infection following surgery is that of Joseph Lister, an Englishman who lived from 1827 to 1912.

The danger of infection is always present in operations. With the opening of the skin, the body's normal protection against infections is weakened. Before Lister, it was believed that the air itself caused an open wound to become infected. Lister realized that infections were caused by germs in the air. He sprayed carbolic

SURGERY

acid on the open wounds to destroy the germs. This was the beginning of antiseptic treatment.

Today, surgery has gone far beyond this and developed aseptic techniques. That is, germs are kept out of the operating room. All equipment is sterilized. In addition to aseptic techniques, many drugs are available to prevent and treat infections.

The use of anesthesia, aseptic techniques, knowledge of the human body, and better surgical methods and tools have made surgery a field with limitless possibilities for saving human lives.

Today a surgeon may safely remove a lung, take out most of the stomach, or operate directly on the human heart. He can open the brain or replace large blood vessels.

All doctors get some training in surgery. But in the past 150 years modern surgery has become so vast a field that doctors must take at least four or five additional years of special study to become surgeons.

When an operation takes place in a modern hospital many preparations are made beforehand. The floors of the operating room are scrubbed. The operating table, which can be raised, lowered, or tilted in any direction, is cleaned, and sterile linen is put on it. A stand holding a tray is placed close to the operating table. The sterilized tools that will be needed

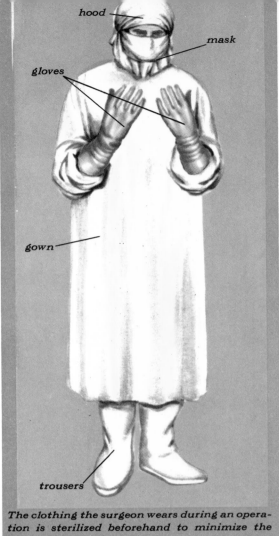

The clothing the surgeon wears during an operation is sterilized beforehand to minimize the danger of infection.

This is an operating room. The operating table (1) can be tilted in any direction depending on the operation to be done. The center lamp (2) is very bright. It lights up the room without casting any shadows. The table for instruments (3) varies in size according to the number of tools needed for the operation. A special machine (4) is used for giving the patient anesthesia. Soiled sponges are put into a receptacle (5). The anesthetist keeps records of the condition of the patient at a special table (6). In some hospitals, television apparatus (7) is attached to the lamp over the operating table so students may observe the operation.

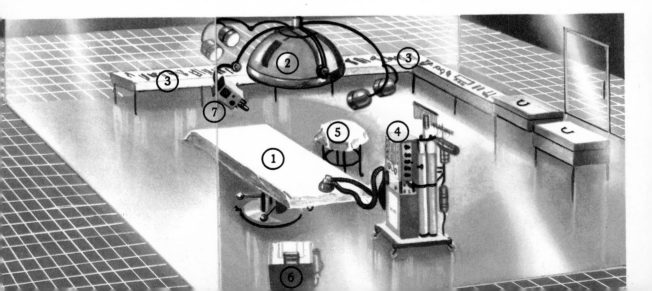

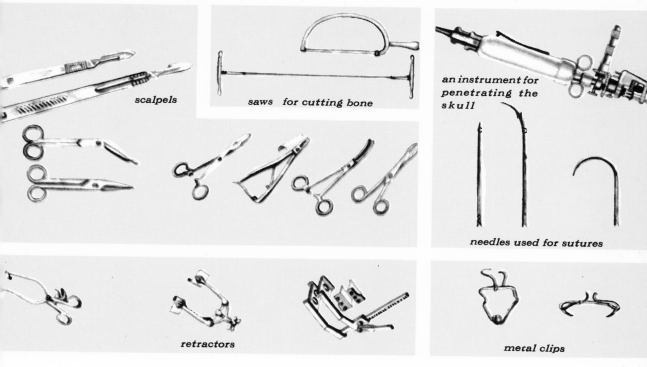

scalpels

saws   for cutting bone

an instrument for penetrating the skull

needles used for sutures

retractors

metal clips

These are some of the instruments used by a surgeon.

during the operation are put there. Other sterilized instruments that may be needed in case of an emergency during the operation are put on a special table in the operating room.

At every operation in a hospital there is a surgical team. It is made up of a surgeon, an assistant doctor, an anesthetist, and a nurse. For difficult cases more doctors and nurses are needed. The surgical team scrub their hands and forearms with a special soap and put on rubber gloves. The doctors and nurses wear sterilized gowns over their clothing, cover their hair with caps, cover their noses and mouths with masks, and wear special shoes.

The patient is wheeled into the operating room and placed on the operating table.

The anesthetist takes the patient's blood pressure and pulse. He watches these closely during the entire operation. He then starts to give the patient anesthesia.

The area that will be operated on is cleansed and an antiseptic put on it. Then the nurse covers the patient with sheets, leaving this area exposed.

The surgeon cuts an opening in the skin with a special knife, called a scalpel. The cut is called the incision. He clamps the arteries and veins to stop bleeding and absorbs extra blood with surgical sponges. He deepens the incision to expose the diseased area. The surgeon holds back the tissues with retractors in order to see the area better. Now the surgeon is ready to perform the actual operation.

When the surgeon is finished, he ties off the blood vessels with suture, a special thread, to prevent them from bleeding. The thread can be made of catgut, silk, cotton, nylon, or fine stainless steel wire. The assistant doctor can then take the clamps off the blood vessels. The retractors are removed and the layers of tissue are brought together and sewn with sutures. The skin is sewn together and, finally, the wound is covered with a bandage.

The patient is then taken to a recovery room. He is kept there, closely watched by nurses, until he is fully awake from the anesthetic. Then he goes back to his room in the hospital, where he is cared for by his surgeon, doctors, and nurses until he is well and ready to go home.

A rice grower
seeding his fields

Laoag

Vigan

Ilagan

SIERRA MADRE

Lingayen

Baler

Quezon City

★ Quezon City
■ Manila

REPUBLIC OF THE PHILIPPINES
AREA: *115,750 square miles*
POP: *24,000,000*
CAPITAL: *Quezon City*
RELIGIONS: *Roman Catholic, Aglepayan*
   (Independent Philippine Catholic),
   Moslem, Protestant
LANGUAGES: *English, Tagalog (official*
   language), Spanish, Visayan,
   Ilokano, Bikol
MONETARY UNIT: *Peso (50c)*

South China Sea

L U Z O N

CATANDUANES

Naga

MOUNT MAYON
▲ 7,926 FT

Legaspi

Calapan

MINDORO

Sibuyan
Sea

Masbate

Calbayog

CALAMIAN ISLANDS

MASBATE

SAMAR

Capiz

Ormoc

LEYTE

PANAY

Iloilo

Bacolod

Baybay

Cebu

CEBU

Taytay

Sulu
Sea

NEGROS

Surigao

PALAWAN

Puerto Princesa

Aborlan

BOHOL

Dumaguete

Mindanao Sea

This chapel was erected on the island of
Cebu at the spot where Magellan was supposed to have landed in 1521.

Cagayan

Dapitan

Malaybalay

M I N D A N A O

Cotabato

Dava

Zamboanga

9,690 FT ▲
MOUNT APO

BASILAN

C e l e b e s
S e a

P
A
C
I
F
I
C
O
C
E
A
N

Scale of Miles

0   50   100

794

The Philippine Islands

The islands of the Republic of the Philippines are so numerous that if a traveler were to spend a day on each one, his trip would take almost 20 years. Actually, of the more than

Manila, the republic's largest city, has many modern buildings, including the town hall in the foreground.

7,000 islands and islets that make up the Republic, less than 500 have an area of more than one square mile. The most important islands are Luzon, Mindanao, Samar, Negros, Palawan, Panay, Mindoro, Leyte, and Cebu.

The island group is located about 500 miles off the coast of southeastern Asia in the Pacific Ocean. The Philippines extend more than 1,100 miles from north to south and almost 700 miles from east to west. They cover about 115,000 square miles. They are the visible peaks of a submerged volcanic mountain chain. The highest volcanic peak is Mount Apo. It rises 9,690 feet above sea level and is located on the island of Mindanao. Mount Mayon, on Luzon, is almost 8,000 feet high. One of the deepest ocean trenches in the world, the Mindanao Trench, lies off the island of Mindanao. The deepest part of it, discovered in 1960, is 36,198 feet deep.

The capital of the Philippines is Quezon City, on the island of Luzon. Quezon City is named after the Islands' first president, Manuel Quezon, who was elected in 1935. The largest city, however, is Manila, with a population of 1,200,000. All the major cities of the Philippines are seaports. The first sailors who visited the islands did not go far inland, but founded communities on the seacoast which gradually grew to become important cities.

The climate of the Philippines is tropical, with little difference in temperature between summer and winter. It is rainy all year long in the south, but there is a short dry season in the north. The seasons are punctuated by typhoons and floods. The typhoons often destroy houses and farmlands.

There are no large rivers on the islands and farmers must depend on rain to water their fields. Dense forests cover much of the land and there are many mountainous areas. Only about 20 percent of the land can be farmed.

Although Chinese traders had probably traveled to the Philippines as early as the 10th century, the first European explorer to discover the islands was Ferdinand Magellan in 1521. His voyage around the world ended in the Philippines, where he was killed in a local tribal battle. Other European sailors visited the islands in the next few years, and one of them, a Spaniard, named the islands for Philip II, the king of Spain. In 1564, another Spaniard, Lopez de Legaspi, came over with troops and began the conquest of the more important islands. He founded the city of Manila in 1571, and in the years that followed, Philippine trade was established with Portugal, Holland, and England.

During the next two centuries the Spaniards maintained their control over the islands. There were some revolts during this period, but very little was achieved by them. When war started between Spain and the United States in 1898, the Philippine leaders welcomed American aid against the Spanish rulers. The Spanish-American War ended quickly with victory for the United States, and the Philippines were bought for $20,000,000.

Although the United States planned to give the Philippines their independence, and began to prepare them for self-government, local leaders wanted the islands to be made independent immediately. This caused some bad feeling between the United States and the Philippines. Finally, in 1935, the islands achieved self-government, although they remained under the guidance of the United States.

In the same year, General Douglas MacArthur went to the Philippines to help prepare against possible invasion by the Japanese. The Japanese attacked Pearl Harbor without warning on December 7, 1941, and the Philippines were soon captured. The Philippine government continued in exile in Washington until the islands were liberated in 1945. They were given their independence in 1946. Philippine Independence Day is July 4, just as it is in the United States.

There are many races in the Philippines. The Negritos, who are pygmies, mostly live primitively in the forests. There are only a few of them left. The Indonesians, from Asia, replaced most of the Negritos centuries ago, but they too are now a minor part of the population. The Filipinos, who in turn forced the Indonesians out of the best parts of the islands, are now the dominant group. About 70 different dialects are spoken in the Philippines, but the official language is a new one based on Tagalog and called Tagalog. English and Spanish are widely spoken, too.

Rice and corn are the main food products of the islands. However, so much rice is needed in the Philippines that some has to be imported. Sugar cane, hemp, coconuts, and tobacco are also grown, as well as fruit, nuts, and coffee.

There are almost 2,000 different types of fish in the waters off the coast of the Philippines, and fish are an important part of the diet. There are more than 3,000 varieties of trees on the islands. Many hardwood trees are cut down for their valuable lumber. Trees also contain cellulose, which is used in the manufacture of plastics. Ropes made from Manila hemp are outstanding for their strength.

Livestock is raised, mostly pigs and cattle. The most useful animal of the islands is the carabao, or water buffalo, which is used for transportation and other jobs for which horses are used in the United States.

Mineral deposits on the islands include gold, silver, iron, and copper. There is not yet much manufacturing in the Philippines. Most of the industries already established process the products that are grown, such as sugar cane, coconuts, tobacco, and rice.

Mt. Mayon is an 8,000 foot volcano on the island of Luzon.

Fishing villages like this one provide one of the basic foods of the islands.

TIME CHART VOLUME 9

represents all time from the beginning of the earth to the present, which is calculated by most authorities to be four to six billion years. The lowest band covers a period of 1,000 years, counting back from the present to A.D. 1000. The band above it covers 4,000 years, counting back from the year A.D. 1000 to 5,000 years ago. Each band represents about four times as many years as the band directly below it. The third band covers 16,000 years, the one above it 64,000 years, and so on. As you go back in time, dates become more and more uncertain. Dates before recorded history—about 3000 B.C.—are the calculations and expert guesses of archeologists and geologists.

Oceans form and cool enough for first life

4,000,000,000 TO 6,000,000,000 YEARS AGO

One-celled animals and plants   Land plants

1,000,000,000
3 OR MORE GLACIAL ERAS
350,000,000 EACH LASTING
Beginning and end of the dinosaurs
100,000,000 ABOUT ONE MILLION YEARS
Age of Mammals
20,000,000

5,000,000

Early man makes his first fire and first implements

1,250,000

350,000

LAST GLACIAL ERA

Development of Stone Age man

90,000

Cave paintings and pictures carved on bone tools

20,000

Ur, first city, has gold and copper

Earliest glass objects, p. 773   Egyptian pyramids

5,000 YEARS AGO
= 3000 B.C.

Constellations grouped and named, p. 712   2000 B.C.

1000 B.C.

Height of Greek civilization   Nebuchadnezzar rules Babylon, p. 751
Birth of Christ
Galen, p. 776   A.D. 1 B.C.   Height of Roman civilization   Romans invade Gaul, p. 718

Roman Empire is divided, p. 736   Height of The Byzantine Empire, p. 736
A.D. 1000   Charles Martel defeats the Moslems, p. 718

DARK AGES

1097   First Crusade
Genghis Khan   1206

1300   First gunpowder

Byzantine Empire falls to the Turks, p. 736   1460   First printing, first type   RENAISSANCE
Columbus   1492
Copernicus revolutionizes astronomy, p. 712   First voyage around the world, p. 739

Catherine the Great made Empress of Russia, p. 770   1698   First steam engine
Thomas Jefferson, p. 743   The French Revolution begins, p. 718
Napoleon becomes Emperor, p. 718
Antarctica discovered, p. 746
Germans invade France, p. 718   South Pole reached, p. 746   Atomic energy   1942
Sputnik I launched, p. 756
A.D. 2000

The type in red with page numbers (such as p. 756) refers to Titles and facts in this volume. Items in black are chosen from the complete chronology in Volume 16 to help place events.

EACH BAND COVERS FOUR TIMES AS MANY YEARS AS THE BAND BELOW IT

16,000 YEARS   4,000 YEARS   1,000 YEARS

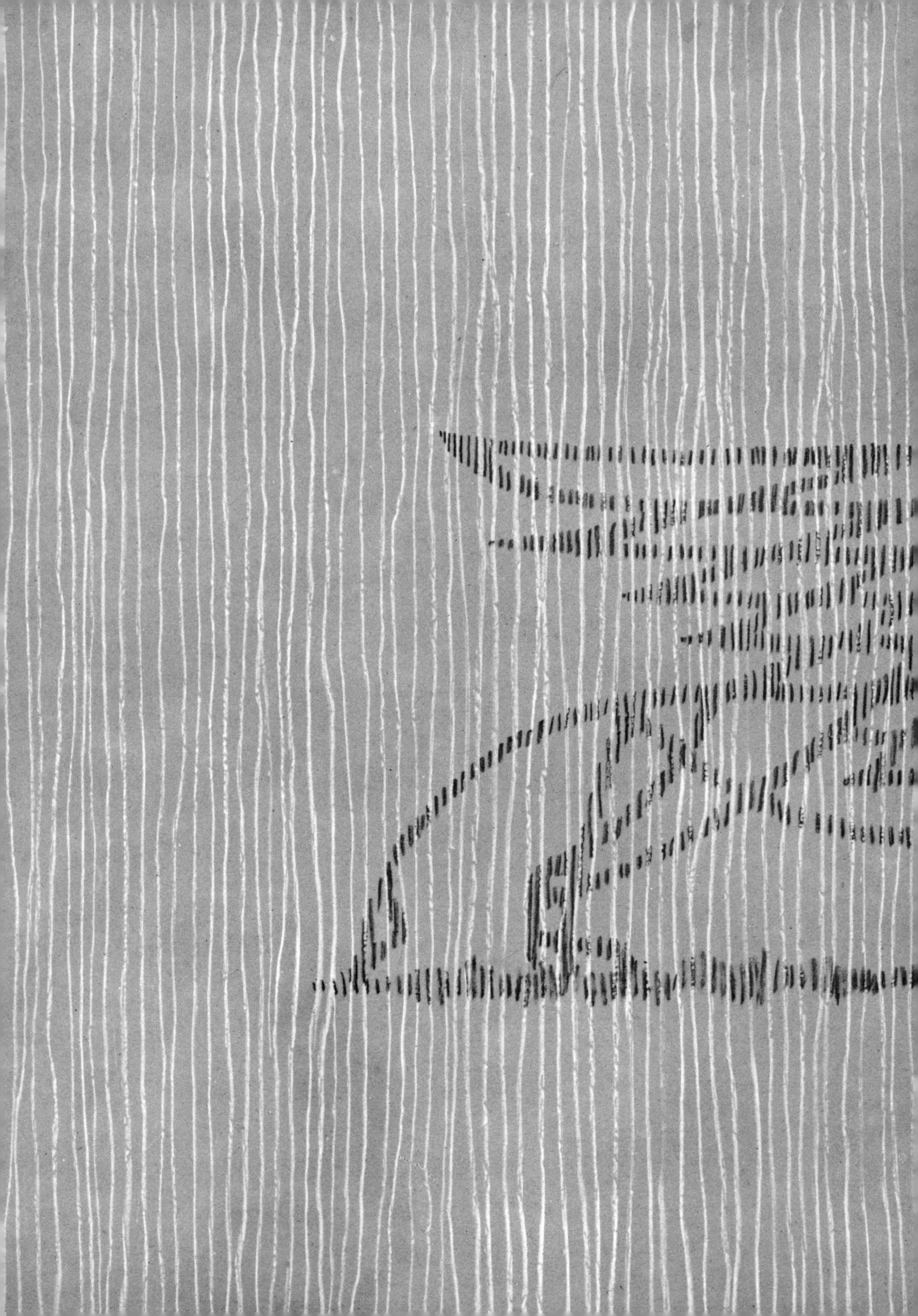